Does a Hot Elf Live NEXT DOOR to You?

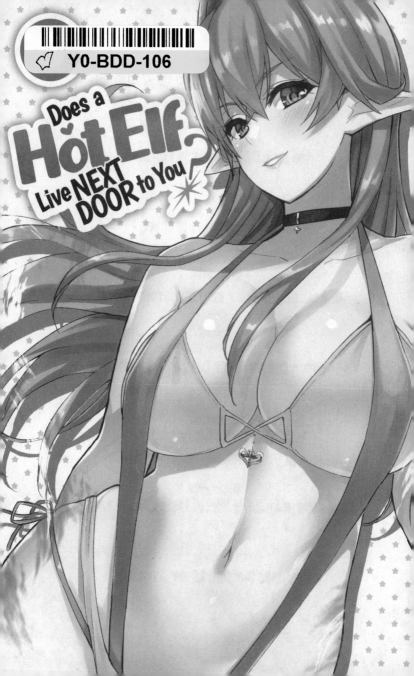

✦ CONTENTS ✦

Chapter 17
Can Love Be Generously Stolen?
-3-

Chapter 18
Does "Size: L" Stand For Lovely?
-25-

Chapter 19
Do the Stars Beat for Love?
-47-

Chapter 20
Which Comes First? Love or the Kiss?
-69-

Chapter 21
Is There a Scramble at School?
-91-

Chapter 22
Does the Neighbor's Secret Taste Like Honey?
-113-

Chapter 23
Should We Blame It All on Summer?
-135-

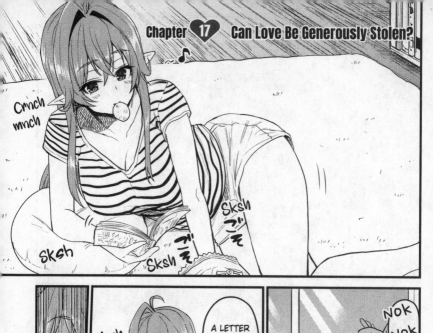

Crnch mnch

Sksh

Sksh Sksh

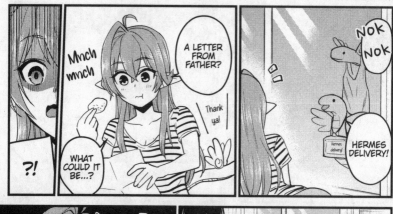

Mnch mnch

A LETTER FROM FATHER?

Thank ya!

WHAT COULD IT BE...?

?!

NOK NOK

HERMES DELIVERY!

Hermes delivery

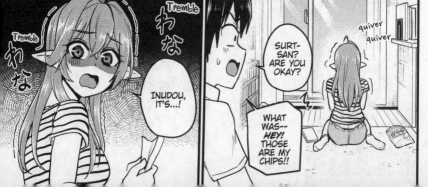

Tremble

Tremble

INUDOU, IT'S...!

SURT-SAN? ARE YOU OKAY?

quiver quiver

WHAT WAS-- HEY! THOSE ARE MY CHIPS!!

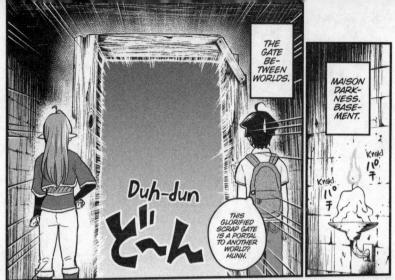

THE GATE BE-TWEEN WORLDS.

MAISON DARK-NESS. BASE-MENT.

Krak! パチ

Krak! パチ

Duh-dun ど~ん

THIS GLORIFIED SCRAP GATE IS A PORTAL TO ANOTHER WORLD? HUINH.

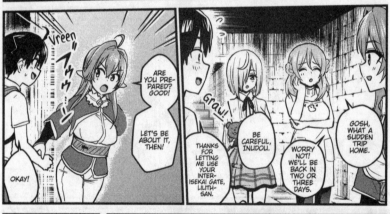

Vreen フゥゥ...

Graw!

ARE YOU PRE-PARED? GOOD!

LET'S BE ABOUT IT, THEN!

OKAY!

THANKS FOR LETTING ME USE YOUR INTER-ISEKAI GATE, LILITH-SAN.

BE CAREFUL, INUDOU.

WORRY NOT! WE'LL BE BACK IN TWO OR THREE DAYS.

GOSH, WHAT A SUDDEN TRIP HOME.

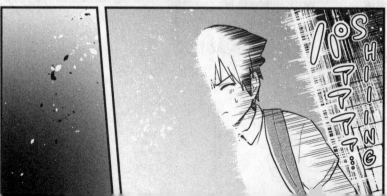

パSHIIING

ぽん
POP
HUH?
Uwaaaaaaaaah!
I JUST GOT HERE AND I'M ALREADY GONNA DIIEEEE!!
CATCH
SHWOOP
Squish
NGH...
THANKS FOR THE CATCH, SURT--

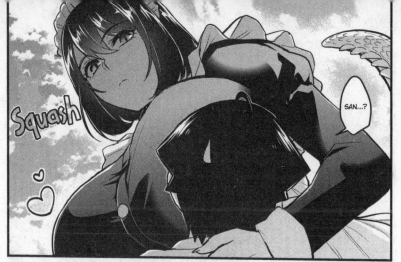

SAN...?

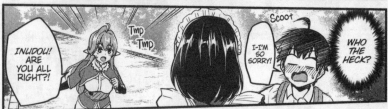

INUDOU!! ARE YOU ALL RIGHT?!

Tmp Tmp

Scoot

I-I'M SO SORRY!

WHO THE HECK?

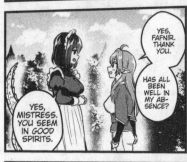

YES, FAFNIR. THANK YOU.

HAS ALL BEEN WELL IN MY ABSENCE?

YES, MISTRESS. YOU SEEM IN GOOD SPIRITS.

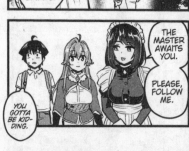

THE MASTER AWAITS YOU.

PLEASE, FOLLOW ME.

YOU GOTTA BE KIDDING.

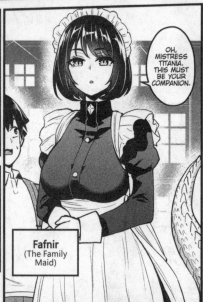

OH, MISTRESS TITANIA. THIS MUST BE YOUR COMPANION.

Fafnir
(The Family Maid)

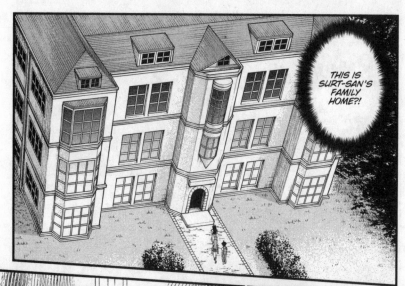

THIS IS SURT-SAN'S FAMILY HOME?!

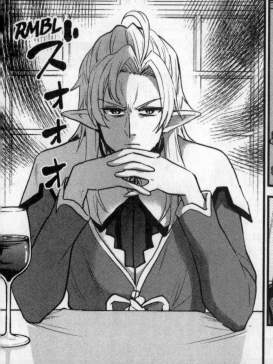

RMBL

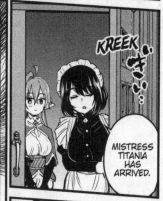

KREEK

MISTRESS TITANIA HAS ARRIVED.

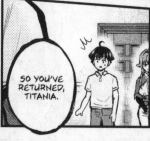

SO YOU'VE RETURNED, TITANIA.

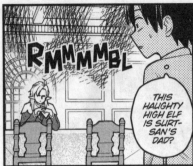

RMMMMBL

THIS HAUGHTY HIGH ELF IS SURT-SAN'S DAD?

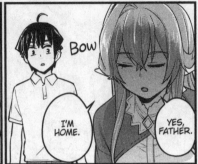

Bow

I'M HOME.

YES, FATHER.

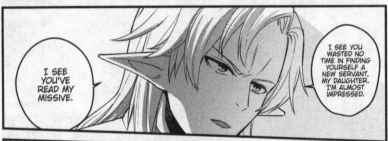

I SEE YOU'VE READ MY MISSIVE.

I SEE YOU WASTED NO TIME IN FINDING YOURSELF A NEW SERVANT, MY DAUGHTER. I'M ALMOST IMPRESSED.

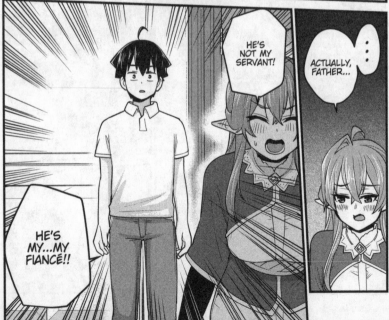

HE'S NOT MY SERVANT!

ACTUALLY, FATHER...

HE'S MY...MY FIANCÉ!!

HER WHAT??!!
BWAAAASH
WHOA! WHAT THE HECK?!
RMMBL
RMMBL
DO MY EARS DECEIVE ME?
RMMBL
MY DAUGHTER IS BETROTHED TO A HUMAN MAN-CHILD?!
RMMBL
RMMBL
EEEP!
IT'S NEWS TO ME TOO, DAD!
FATHER, NO!
TWITCH
I SPEAK THE TRUTH!

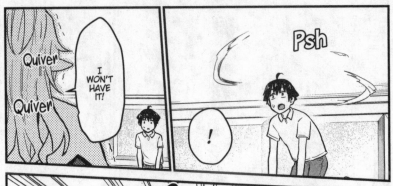

Quiver

Quiver

I WON'T HAVE IT!

!

Psh

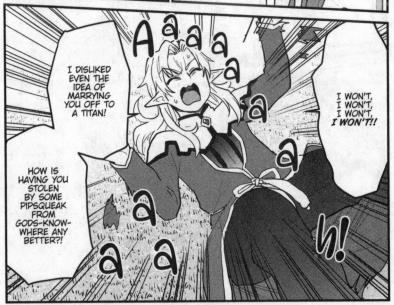

Aaaaaaa aaaah!

I DISLIKED EVEN THE IDEA OF MARRYING YOU OFF TO A TITAN!

HOW IS HAVING YOU STOLEN BY SOME PIPSQUEAK FROM GODS-KNOW-WHERE ANY BETTER?!

I WON'T, I WON'T, I WON'T, *I WON'T!!*

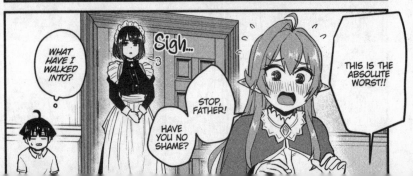

WHAT HAVE I WALKED INTO?

Sigh...

STOP, FATHER!

HAVE YOU NO SHAME?

THIS IS THE ABSOLUTE WORST!!

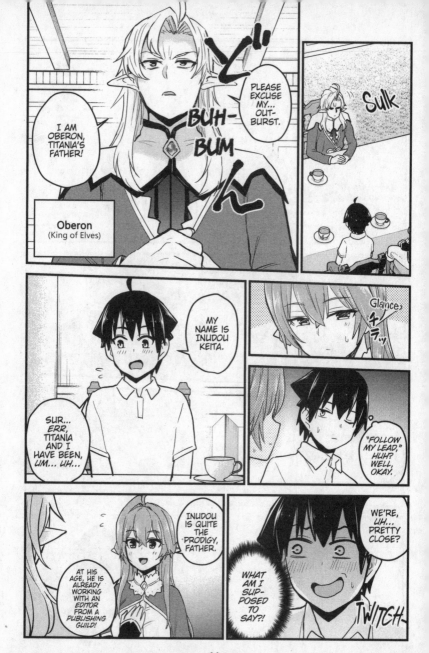

PLEASE EXCUSE MY... OUTBURST.

I AM OBERON, TITANIA'S FATHER!

BUH-BUM

Oberon
(King of Elves)

Sulk

MY NAME IS INUDOU KEITA.

Glance

SUR... ERR, TITANIA AND I HAVE BEEN, UM... UH...

"FOLLOW MY LEAD," HUH? WELL, OKAY.

INUDOU IS QUITE THE PRODIGY, FATHER.

AT HIS AGE, HE IS ALREADY WORKING WITH AN EDITOR FROM A PUBLISHING GUILD!

WHAT AM I SUPPOSED TO SAY?!

WE'RE, UH... PRETTY CLOSE?

TWITCH

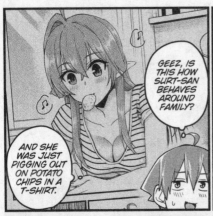

GEEZ, IS THIS HOW SURT-SAN BEHAVES AROUND FAMILY?

AND SHE WAS JUST PIGGING OUT ON POTATO CHIPS IN A T-SHIRT.

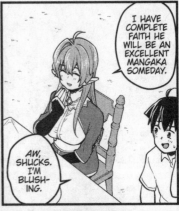

I HAVE COMPLETE FAITH HE WILL BE AN EXCELLENT MANGAKA SOMEDAY.

AW, SHUCKS. I'M BLUSHING.

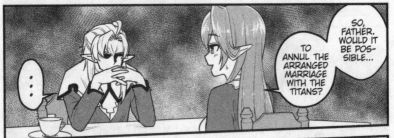

SO, FATHER, WOULD IT BE POSSIBLE...

TO ANNUL THE ARRANGED MARRIAGE WITH THE TITANS?

· · ·

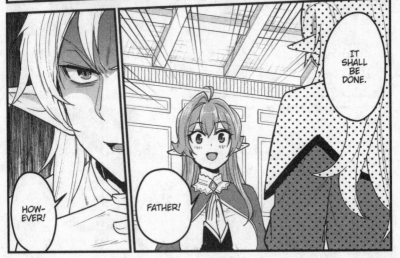

IT SHALL BE DONE.

HOWEVER!

FATHER!

IF IT IS TRUE THAT THIS MAN IS YOUR FIANCÉ...
FWIP
THEN I DEMAND YOU SHOW ME PROOF! HERE AND NOW!
PROOF?!
HE CAME HERE SO YOU MIGHT MEET HIM! WHAT MORE IS THERE TO PROVE?!
SOMETHING ABOUT HIS BEHAVIOR STRIKES ME AS...
SUSPICIOUS.

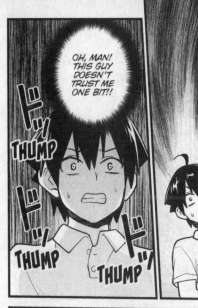

OH, MAN! THIS GUY DOESN'T TRUST ME ONE BIT!!

THUMP

THUMP

THUMP

THUMP

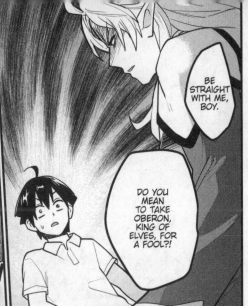

BE STRAIGHT WITH ME, BOY.

DO YOU MEAN TO TAKE OBERON, KING OF ELVES, FOR A FOOL?!

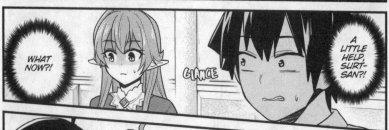

WHAT NOW?!

GLANCE

A LITTLE HELP, SURT-SAN?!

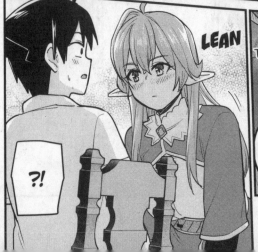

LEAN

?!

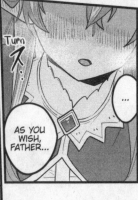

Turn

...

AS YOU WISH, FATHER...

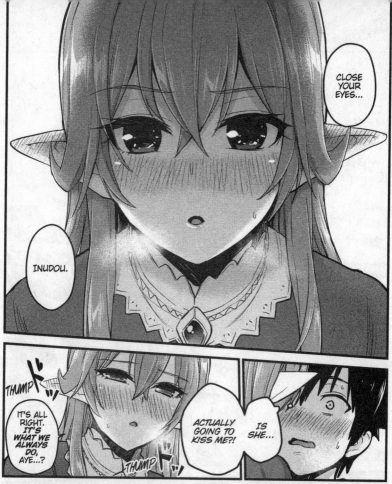

CLOSE YOUR EYES...

INUDOU.

IT'S ALL RIGHT. IT'S WHAT WE ALWAYS DO, AYE...?

ACTUALLY GOING TO KISS ME?!

IS SHE...

THUMP

THUMP

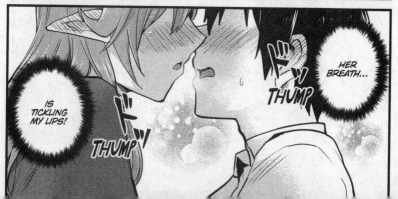

HER BREATH...

IS TICKLING MY LIPS!

THUMP

THUMP

OH NO YOU DON'T!!
FWSH
BWASH
GAH!!
わな Trmbl
わな Trmbl
WHAT YOU ALWAYS DO...?!
YOU ALWAYS... ALWAYS...
NOOO! YOUR FATHER WON'T STAND FOR THIS!!
だっ ZWOOM

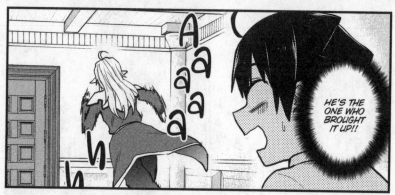

HE'S THE ONE WHO BROUGHT IT UP!!

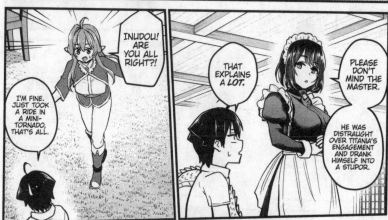

INUDOU! ARE YOU ALL RIGHT?!

I'M FINE. JUST TOOK A RIDE IN A MINI-TORNADO, THAT'S ALL.

THAT EXPLAINS A *LOT.*

PLEASE DON'T MIND THE MASTER.

HE WAS DISTRAUGHT OVER TITANIA'S ENGAGEMENT AND DRANK HIMSELF INTO A STUPOR.

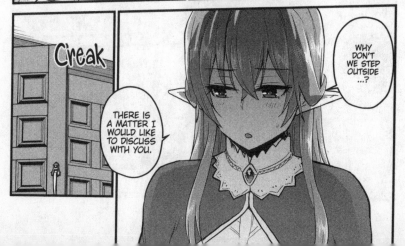

Creak

WHY DON'T WE STEP OUTSIDE...?

THERE IS A MATTER I WOULD LIKE TO DISCUSS WITH YOU.

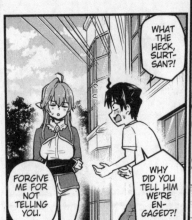

WHAT THE HECK, SURT-SAN?!

WHY DID YOU TELL HIM WE'RE ENGAGED?!

FORGIVE ME FOR NOT TELLING YOU.

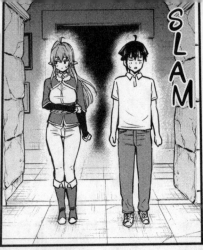

SLAM

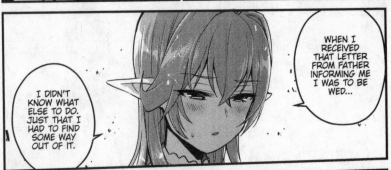

I DIDN'T KNOW WHAT ELSE TO DO. JUST THAT I HAD TO FIND SOME WAY OUT OF IT.

WHEN I RECEIVED THAT LETTER FROM FATHER INFORMING ME I WAS TO BE WED...

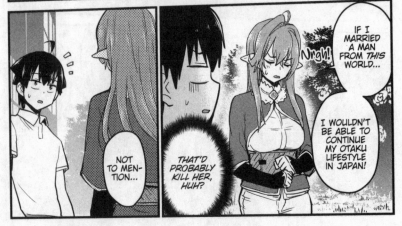

NOT TO MENTION...

THAT'D PROBABLY KILL HER, HUH?

Nrgh!

IF I MARRIED A MAN FROM *THIS* WORLD...

I WOULDN'T BE ABLE TO CONTINUE MY OTAKU LIFESTYLE IN JAPAN!

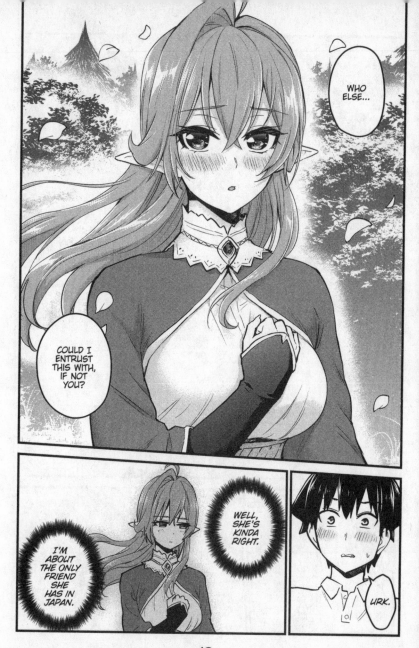

WHO ELSE...

COULD I ENTRUST THIS WITH, IF NOT YOU?

I'M ABOUT THE ONLY FRIEND SHE HAS IN JAPAN.

WELL, SHE'S KINDA RIGHT.

URK.

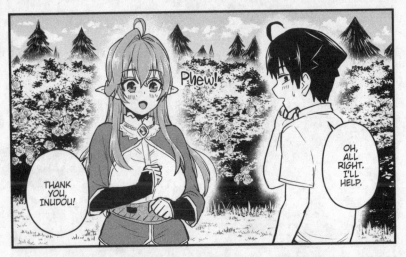

THANK YOU, INUDOU!

PHEW!

OH, ALL RIGHT. I'LL HELP.

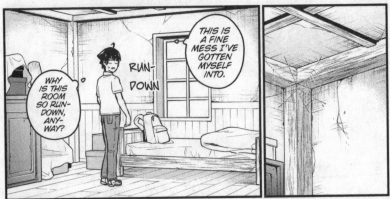

WHY IS THIS ROOM SO RUN-DOWN, ANY-WAY?

RUN-DOWN

THIS IS A FINE MESS I'VE GOTTEN MYSELF INTO.

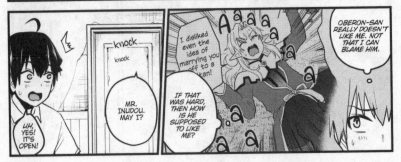

UH, YES! IT'S OPEN!

knock

knock

MR. INUDOU. MAY I?

I disliked even the idea of marrying you off to a human!

AaaAaaa

IF THAT WAS HARD, THEN HOW IS HE SUPPOSED TO LIKE ME?

OBERON-SAN REALLY DOESN'T LIKE ME. NOT THAT I CAN BLAME HIM.

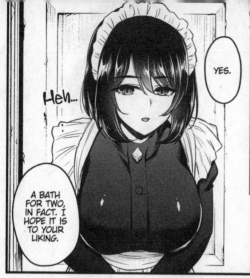

YES.

Heh...

A BATH FOR TWO, IN FACT. I HOPE IT IS TO YOUR LIKING.

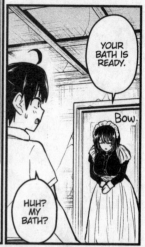

YOUR BATH IS READY.

Bow

HUH? MY BATH?

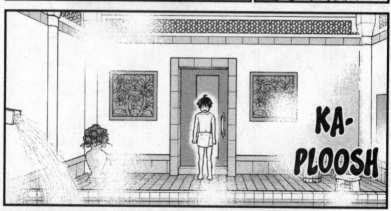

KA-PLOOSH

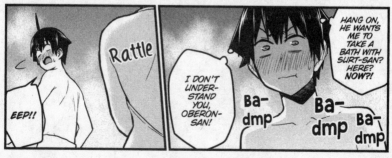

Rattle

EEP!!

I DON'T UNDER-STAND YOU, OBERON-SAN!

HANG ON, HE WANTS ME TO TAKE A BATH WITH SURT-SAN? HERE? NOW?!

Ba-dmp

Ba-dmp

Ba-dmp

ALLOW ME...
TO SCRUB YOUR BACK.
OKAY, NOW I'M OFFICIALLY CONFUSED!!

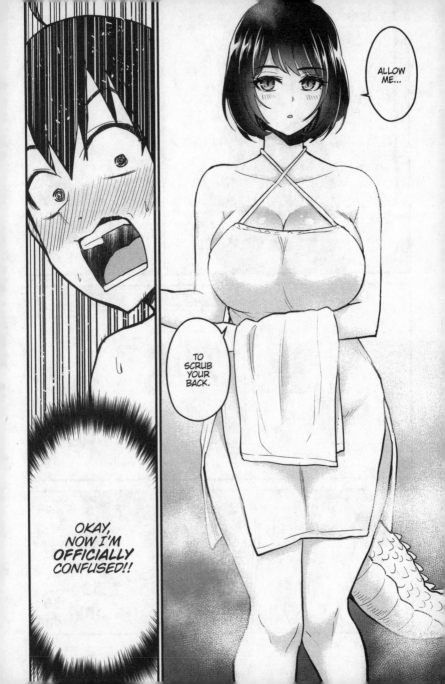

Does a Hot Elf Live NEXT DOOR to You?

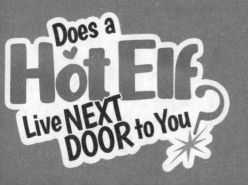

Does a Hot Elf Live NEXT DOOR to You?

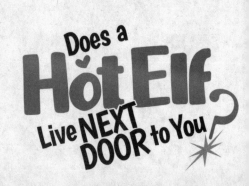

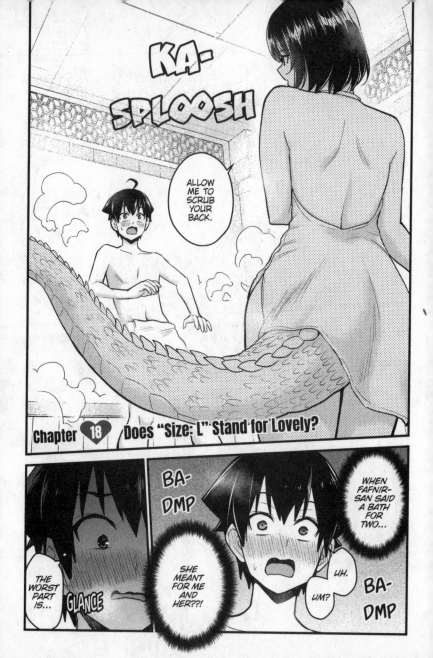

Chapter 18 Does "Size: L" Stand for Lovely?

ばい
BA-
BA-
ん
BOOM
THAT FABRIC IS PAPER-THIN!
A LITTLE WATER AND NOTHING WOULD BE LEFT TO THE IMAGINATION!!
Jiggle
Jiggle
Tight♡
Tight♡
LOOM
ARE YOU QUITE ALL RIGHT?
HUU-WHAT?!
OH, CRAP! SHE SNUCK UP ON ME!

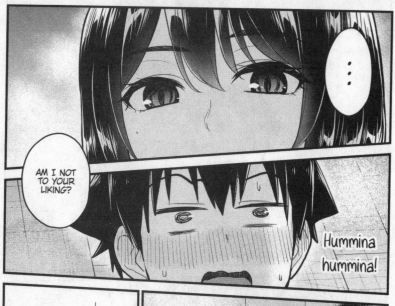

…

AM I NOT TO YOUR LIKING?

Hummina hummina!

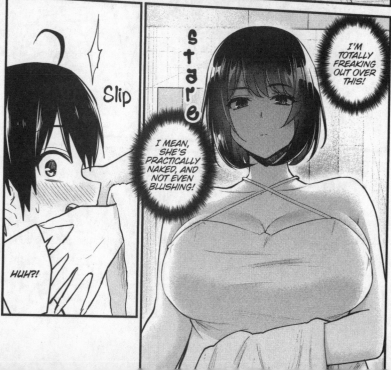

Slip

Stare

HUH?!

I MEAN, SHE'S PRACTICALLY NAKED, AND NOT EVEN BLUSHING!

I'M TOTALLY FREAKING OUT OVER THIS!

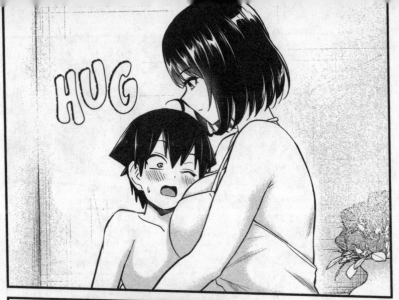

HUG

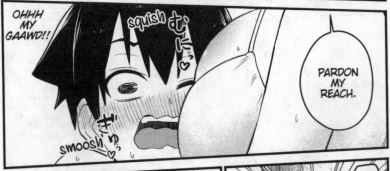

OHHH MY GAAWD!!

squish むに♥

PARDON MY REACH.

smoosh むり♥

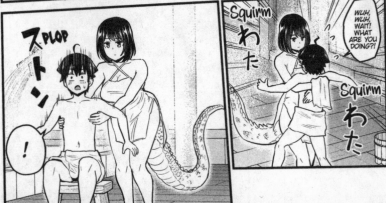

PLOP ズトン

！

Squirm わた

WUH, WUH, WAIT! WHAT ARE YOU DOING?!

Squirm わた

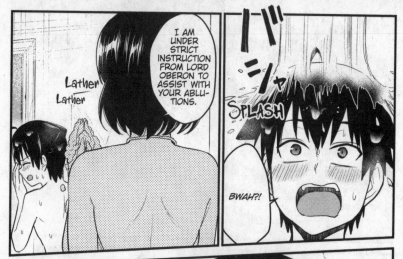

I AM UNDER STRICT INSTRUCTION FROM LORD OBERON TO ASSIST WITH YOUR ABLUTIONS.

Lather
Lather

SPLASH

BWAH?!

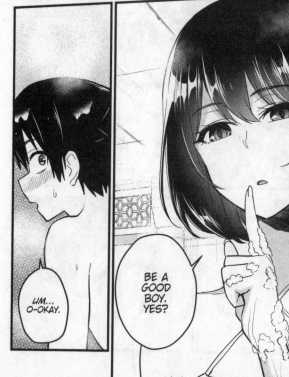

UM... O-OKAY.

BE A GOOD BOY. YES?

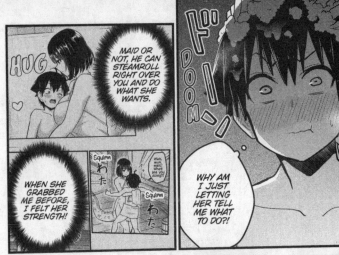

HUG

MAID OR NOT, HE CAN STEAMROLL RIGHT OVER YOU AND DO WHAT SHE WANTS.

WHEN SHE GRABBED ME BEFORE, I FELT HER STRENGTH!

Squirm
わた

Mum, mum, wait! What are you doing?!

Squirm
わた

WHY AM I JUST LETTING HER TELL ME WHAT TO DO?!

HEY, WAIT!!

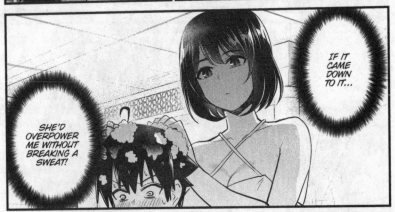

IF IT CAME DOWN TO IT...

SHE'D OVERPOWER ME WITHOUT BREAKING A SWEAT!

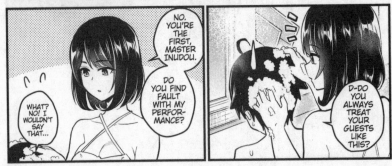

NO. YOU'RE THE FIRST, MASTER INUDOU.

DO YOU FIND FAULT WITH MY PERFOR-MANCE?

WHAT? NO! I WOULDN'T SAY THAT...

D-DO YOU ALWAYS TREAT YOUR GUESTS LIKE THIS?

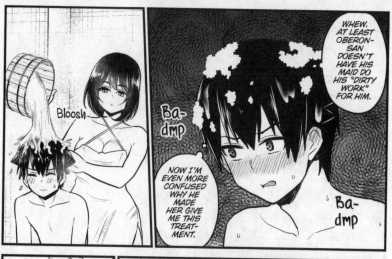

Bloosh

WHEW. AT LEAST OBERON-SAN DOESN'T HAVE HIS MAID DO HIS "DIRTY WORK" FOR HIM.

Ba-dmp

NOW I'M EVEN MORE CONFUSED WHY HE MADE HER GIVE ME THIS TREATMENT.

Ba-dmp

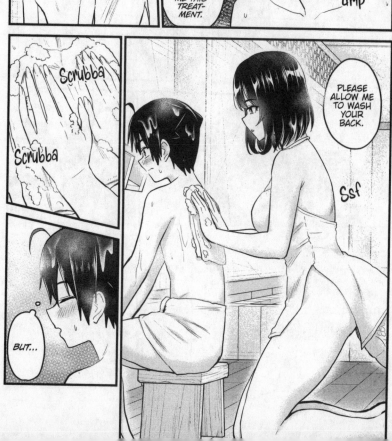

Scrubba

Scrubba

BUT...

PLEASE ALLOW ME TO WASH YOUR BACK.

Ssf

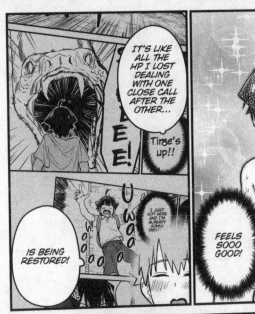

IT'S LIKE ALL THE HP I LOST DEALING WITH ONE CLOSE CALL AFTER THE OTHER...

Time's up!!

I JUST GOT HERE AND I'M ALREADY GONNA DIE!!

IS BEING RESTORED!

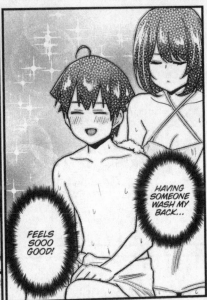

HAVING SOMEONE WASH MY BACK...

FEELS SOOO GOOD!

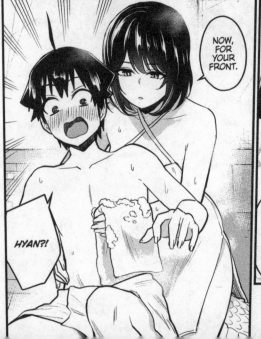

NOW, FOR YOUR FRONT.

HYAN?!

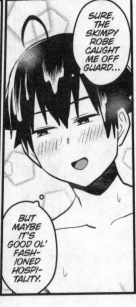

SURE, THE SKIMPY ROBE CAUGHT ME OFF GUARD...

BUT MAYBE IT'S GOOD OL' FASHIONED HOSPITALITY.

H-H-H-HANG ON, STOP!
I CAN DO THIS PART MYSELF, THANK YOU!
CER-TAINLY NOT.
I INTEND TO SEE MY DUTY TO ITS COMPLETION.
Rubba
Rubba
HER JUBBLIES ARE SCRUBBA-SCRUBBING MY BACK, TOO!!

ZZZAP
Pawoo
UH-OH... I KNOW THIS FEELING!
Pawoo
MY SWITCH IS ABOUT TO FLIP!!
MASTER INUDOU.
I CANNOT WASH YOU WHEN YOU HUNCH OVER LIKE THAT.
PERCH
W-WAIT! I-I'M NOT, UM...

たぷ
Bounce
たぷ
Boing
PLEASE RELAX.
Push
Smooosh
AAHHH~~!!
OH NO!!
THIS IS CERTAIN DEATH FOR A... A VIRGIN LIKE ME!
Thump Thump Thump Thump Thump
ドドドドド
ビクッ
Flinch
ズル…
Slip

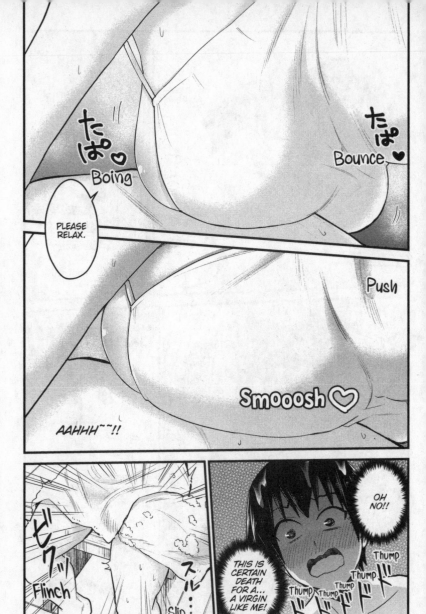

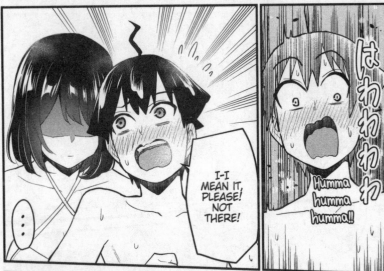

I-I MEAN IT, PLEASE! NOT THERE!

はわわわわ

Humma humma humma!!

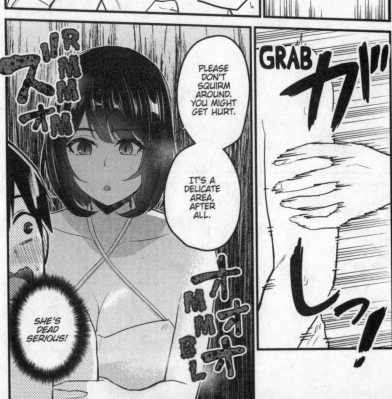

ズ!! RMMM オォ

PLEASE DON'T SQUIRM AROUND. YOU MIGHT GET HURT.

IT'S A DELICATE AREA, AFTER ALL.

GRAB ガ

し!

オォォ MMB L

SHE'S DEAD SERIOUS!

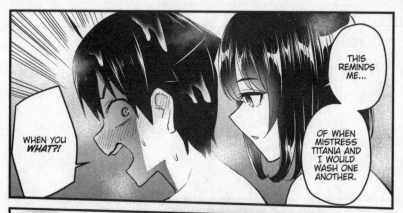

THIS REMINDS ME...

OF WHEN MISTRESS TITANIA AND I WOULD WASH ONE ANOTHER.

WHEN YOU *WHAT?!*

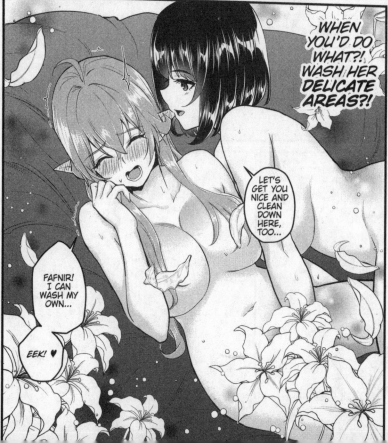

WHEN YOU'D DO WHAT?! WASH HER DELICATE AREAS?!

LET'S GET YOU NICE AND CLEAN DOWN HERE, TOO...

FAFNIR! I CAN WASH MY OWN...

EEK! ♥

ODD.
YOUR SHAPE ISN'T QUITE WHAT I WAS EXPECTING...
FLINCH
THAT'S BECAUSE, UH...!
IT'S BECAUSE YOU'RE TOUCHING IT WITH YOUR BARE HANDS!!
WAIT.
HANDS?
Grasp
Scrubba
Dubba
PLEASE STAY COMPLETELY STILL. I WOULD HATE TO INJURE YOU WITH MY SCALES.
IT WAS HER TAIL?!

Droop
Ploosh
M'KAY...
SQUEAKY CLEAN
THERE. YOU'RE AS CLEAN AS CAN BE.
THANK YOU... VERY MUCH.
MY TALLY-WHACKER GOT MANHAN-DLED BY A TAIL...
YOU KNOW WHAT, IT WAS MY MIND IN THE GUTTER.
Whine
FAFNIR-SAN COULD HAVE BEEN WASHING A PUPPY FOR ALL SHE CARED.
WHAT WOULD YOU LIKE TO DO NOW?
Ssf
Um!
I'M FINE NOW, I'LL JUST--

WAG
WOULD YOU...
LIKE TO MATE WITH ME?

HUH??!
STAND
FORGIVE ME.

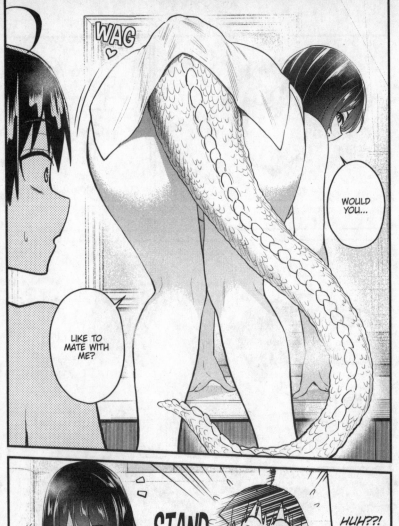

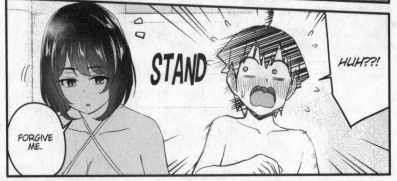

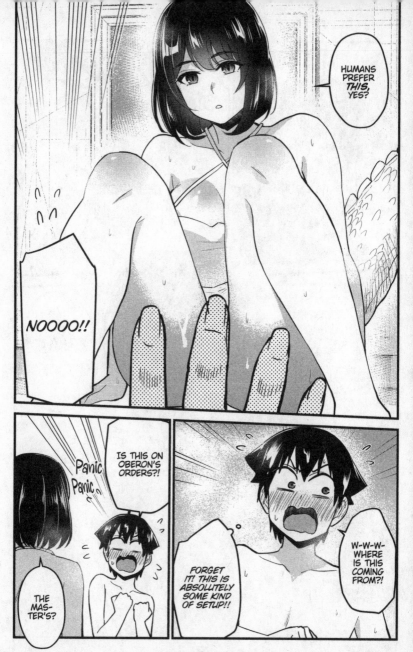

HUMANS PREFER *THIS*, YES?

NOOOO!!

IS THIS ON OBERON'S ORDERS?!

Panic Panic

THE MAS-TER'S?

W-W-W-WHERE IS THIS COMING FROM?!

FORGET IT! THIS IS ABSOLUTELY SOME KIND OF SETUP!!

STAND
NO. I WAS NOT ORDERED TO DO THIS.
SQUEEZE
ぎゅっ
WHUPFF!
FORGIVE MY IMPROPRIETY, MASTER INUDOU...
MGH!!
BUT I HAVE BECOME QUITE ENAMORED WITH YOU.

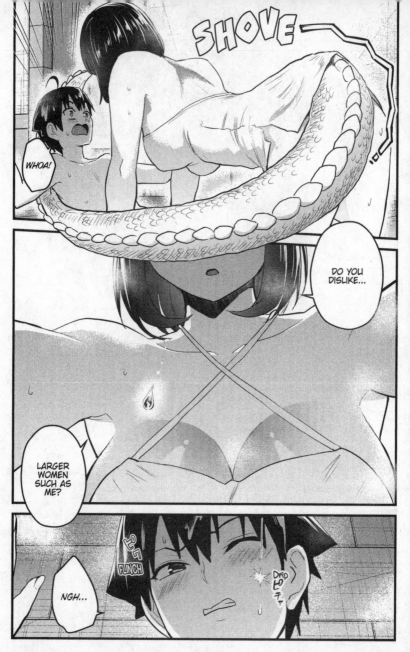

SHOVE

WHOA!

DO YOU DISLIKE...

LARGER WOMEN SUCH AS ME?

NGH...

FLINCH

Drip

— 43 —

Does a Hot Elf Live NEXT DOOR to You?

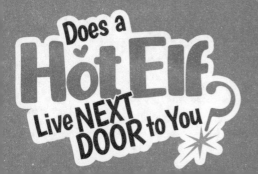

Does a Hot Elf Live NEXT DOOR to You?

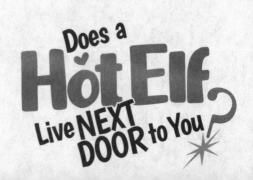

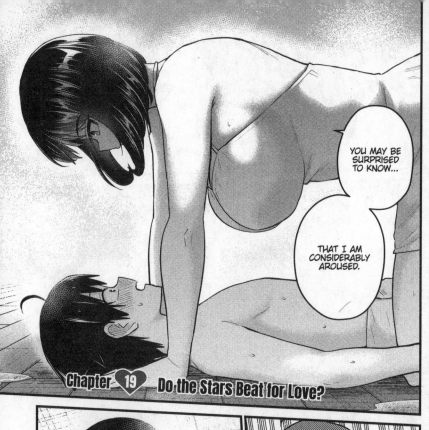

YOU MAY BE SURPRISED TO KNOW...

THAT I AM CONSIDERABLY AROUSED.

Chapter 19 — Do the Stars Beat for Love?

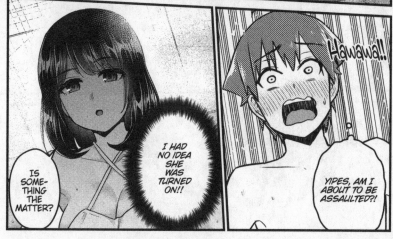

IS SOMETHING THE MATTER?

I HAD NO IDEA SHE WAS TURNED ON!!

Hawawa!!

YIPES, AM I ABOUT TO BE ASSAULTED?!

CHATTER
CHATTER
UM! I, UH...
AM I ABOUT TO LOSE MY VIRGINITY...
TO A MONSTER MUSUME MAID?!
I-I CAN'T.
I CAN'T M-M-MATE WITH YOU.
YOU CAN'T?

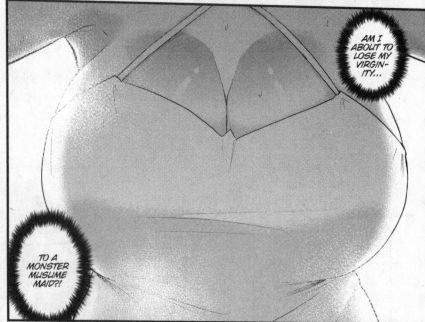

FROM MY UNDER-STANDING, HUMANS ARE IN A PERPETUAL STATE OF HEAT, ARE THEY NOT?
I'M NOT TALKING ABOUT SCIENCE HERE!!
I'M NOT GETTING THROUGH TO HER!!
Isekai folks are scary!!
WHY DO YOU REFUSE ME?
DOES YOUR HEART ALREADY BELONG TO ANOTHER?
HUH?

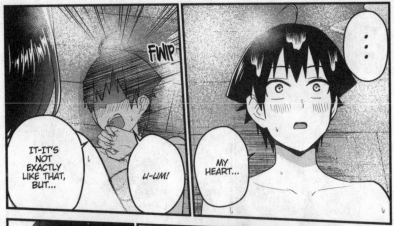

FWIP

IT-IT'S NOT EXACTLY LIKE THAT, BUT...

U-UM!

MY HEART...

...

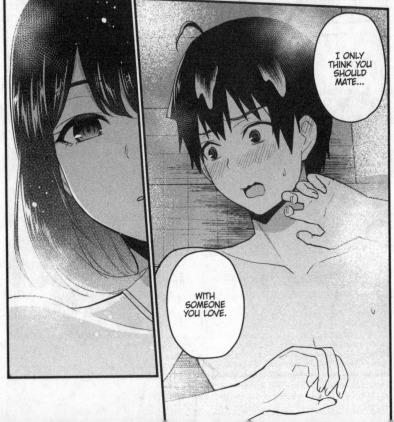

I ONLY THINK YOU SHOULD MATE...

WITH SOMEONE YOU LOVE.

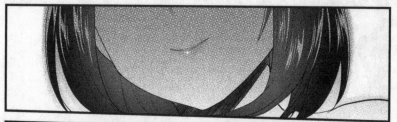

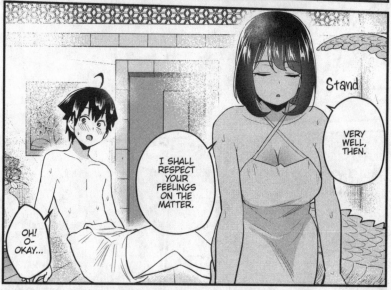

Stand

VERY WELL, THEN.

I SHALL RESPECT YOUR FEELINGS ON THE MATTER.

OH! O-OKAY...

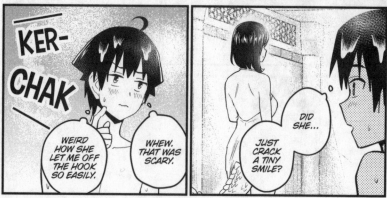

KER-CHAK

WEIRD HOW SHE LET ME OFF THE HOOK SO EASILY.

WHEW. THAT WAS SCARY.

DID SHE...

JUST CRACK A TINY SMILE?

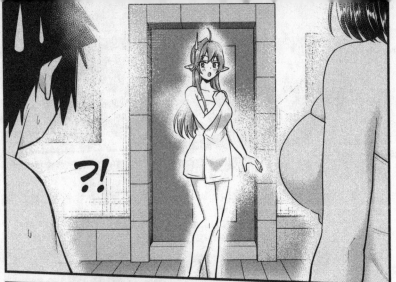

?!

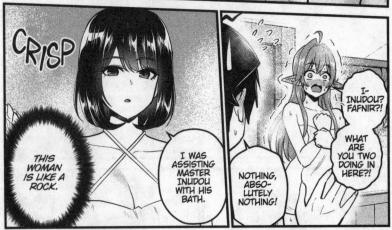

CRISP

THIS WOMAN IS LIKE A ROCK.

I WAS ASSISTING MASTER INUDOU WITH HIS BATH.

NOTHING, ABSO-LUTELY NOTHING!

I- INUDOU? FAFNIR?!

WHAT ARE YOU TWO DOING IN HERE?!

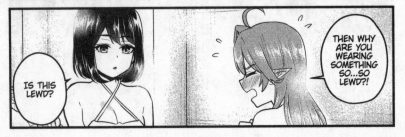

IS THIS LEWD?

THEN WHY ARE YOU WEARING SOMETHING SO...SO LEWD?!

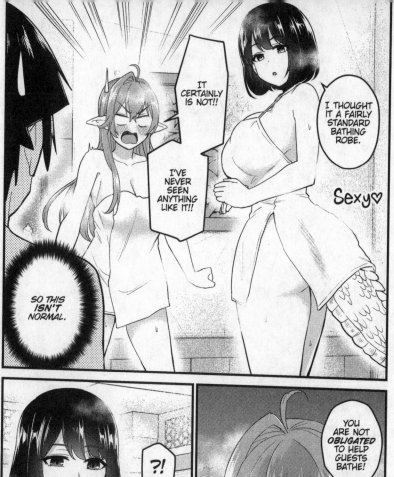

IT CERTAINLY IS NOT!!

I THOUGHT IT A FAIRLY STANDARD BATHING ROBE.

I'VE NEVER SEEN ANYTHING LIKE IT!!

Sexy♡

SO THIS ISN'T NORMAL.

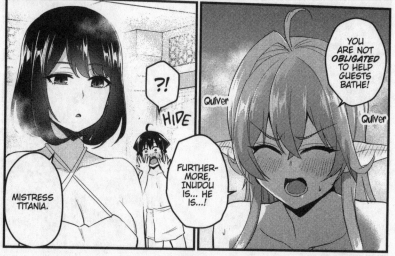

?!

HIDE

MISTRESS TITANIA.

FURTHER-MORE, INUDOU IS... HE IS...!

Quiver

YOU ARE NOT *OBLIGATED* TO HELP GUESTS BATHE!

Quiver

YOU'VE LOST YOUR TOWEL.
Naked♥
Aaaaaaaaaaaaaaah!
SLAM!!
TITANIA?!
I HEARD A SCREAM! ARE YOU--

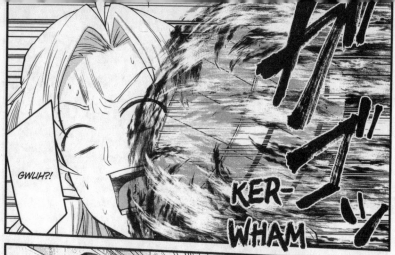

GWUH?!

KER-
WHAM

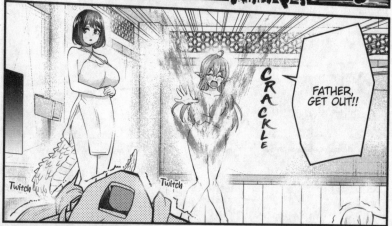

Twitch

Twitch

CRACKLE

FATHER, GET OUT!!

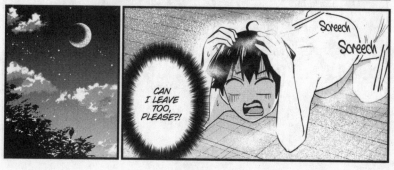

CAN I LEAVE TOO, PLEASE?!

Screech

Screech

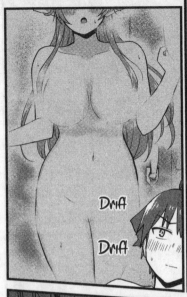

Drift

Drift

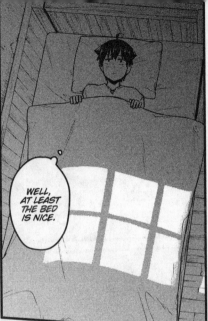

WELL, AT LEAST THE BED IS NICE.

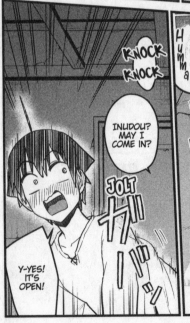

KNOCK KNOCK

INUDOU? MAY I COME IN?

JOLT

Y-YES! IT'S OPEN!

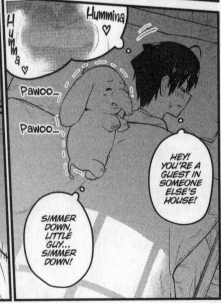

Humma

Hummina ♡

Humma ♡

Pawoo...

Pawoo...

SIMMER DOWN, LITTLE GUY... SIMMER DOWN!

HEY! YOU'RE A GUEST IN SOMEONE ELSE'S HOUSE!

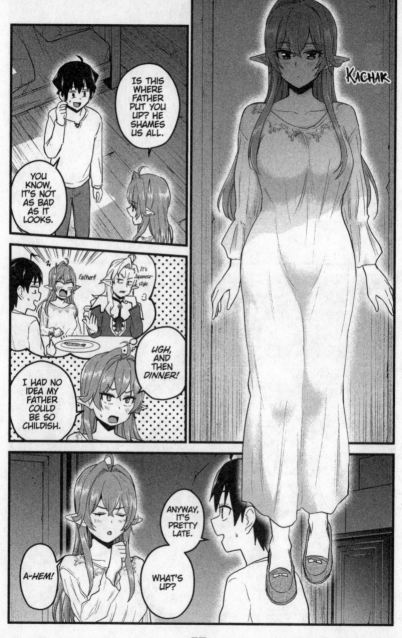

IS THIS WHERE FATHER PUT YOU UP? HE SHAMES US ALL.

YOU KNOW, IT'S NOT AS BAD AS IT LOOKS.

KACHAK

FATHER!!

It's Japanese-style.

UGH, AND THEN DINNER!

I HAD NO IDEA MY FATHER COULD BE SO CHILDISH.

A-HEM!

ANYWAY, IT'S PRETTY LATE.

WHAT'S UP?

— 57 —

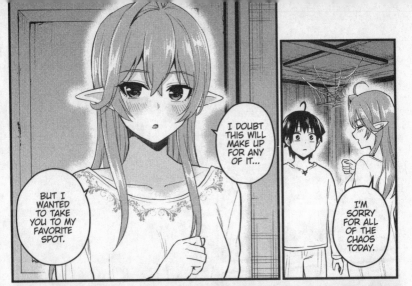

I DOUBT THIS WILL MAKE UP FOR ANY OF IT...

BUT I WANTED TO TAKE YOU TO MY FAVORITE SPOT.

I'M SORRY FOR ALL OF THE CHAOS TODAY.

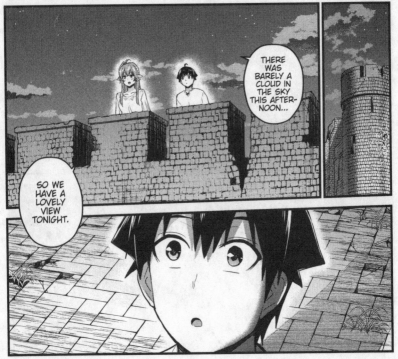

THERE WAS BARELY A CLOUD IN THE SKY THIS AFTERNOON...

SO WE HAVE A LOVELY VIEW TONIGHT.

WOW...
IT'S STRANGE, ISN'T IT?

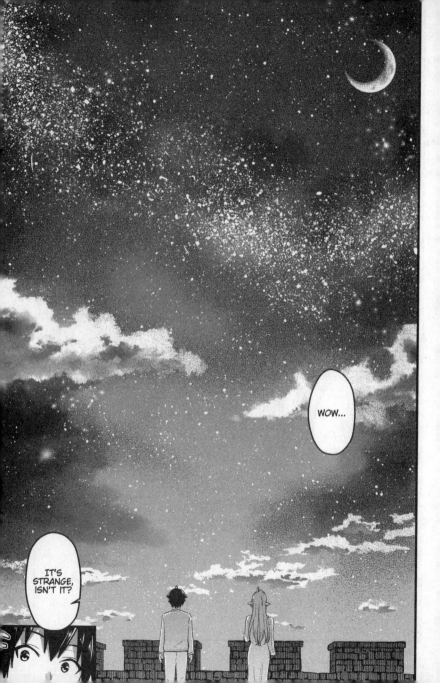

JAPAN IS WORLDS APART FROM THIS PLACE...
BUT SOMEHOW, WE SHARE THE SAME STARS.

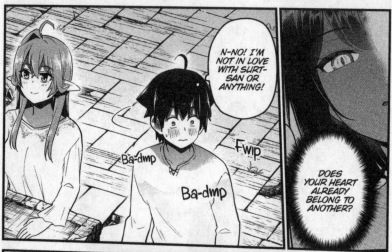

N-NO! I'M NOT IN LOVE WITH SURT-SAN OR ANYTHING!

Ba-dmp

Ba-dmp

Fwip

DOES YOUR HEART ALREADY BELONG TO ANOTHER?

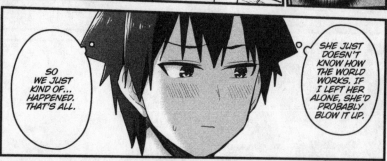

SO WE JUST KIND OF... HAPPENED. THAT'S ALL.

SHE JUST DOESN'T KNOW HOW THE WORLD WORKS. IF I LEFT HER ALONE, SHE'D PROBABLY BLOW IT UP.

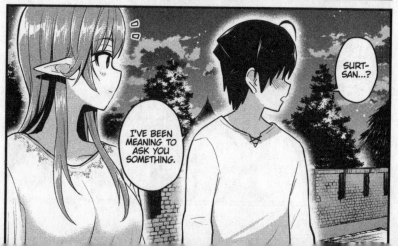

I'VE BEEN MEANING TO ASK YOU SOMETHING.

SURT-SAN...?

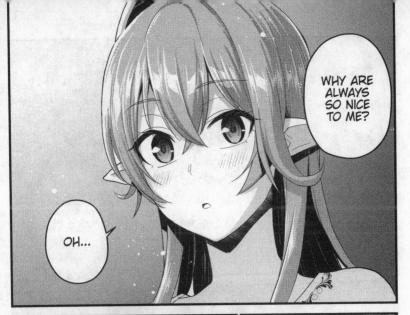

WHY ARE ALWAYS SO NICE TO ME?

OH...

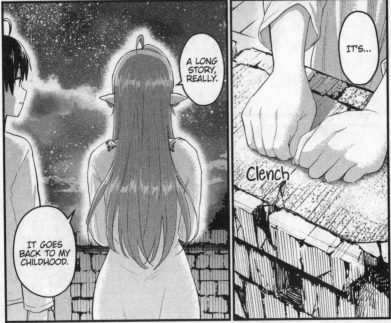

A LONG STORY, REALLY.

IT GOES BACK TO MY CHILDHOOD.

IT'S...

Clench

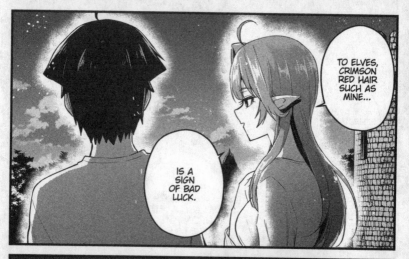

TO ELVES, CRIMSON RED HAIR SUCH AS MINE...

IS A SIGN OF BAD LUCK.

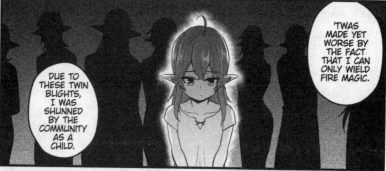

'TWAS MADE YET WORSE BY THE FACT THAT I CAN ONLY WIELD FIRE MAGIC.

DUE TO THESE TWIN BLIGHTS, I WAS SHUNNED BY THE COMMUNITY AS A CHILD.

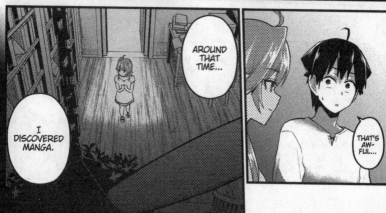

AROUND THAT TIME...

I DISCOVERED MANGA.

THAT'S AW-FUL...

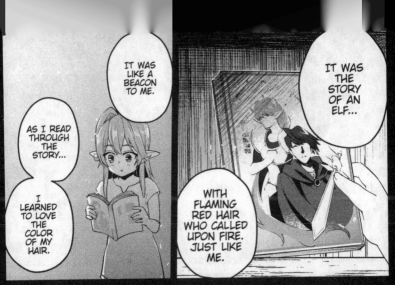

IT WAS THE STORY OF AN ELF...

IT WAS LIKE A BEACON TO ME.

AS I READ THROUGH THE STORY...

I LEARNED TO LOVE THE COLOR OF MY HAIR.

WITH FLAMING RED HAIR WHO CALLED UPON FIRE. JUST LIKE ME.

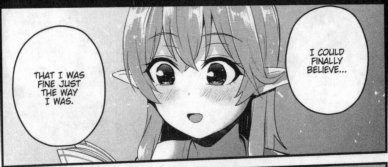

THAT I WAS FINE JUST THE WAY I WAS.

I COULD FINALLY BELIEVE...

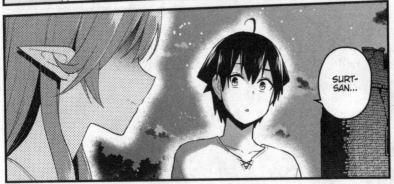

SURT-SAN...

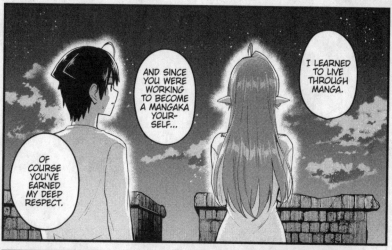

AND SINCE YOU WERE WORKING TO BECOME A MANGAKA YOUR-SELF...

I LEARNED TO LIVE THROUGH MANGA.

OF COURSE YOU'VE EARNED MY DEEP RESPECT.

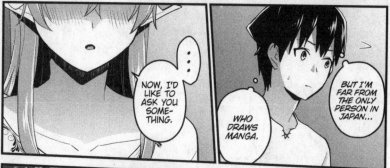

NOW, I'D LIKE TO ASK YOU SOME-THING.

WHO DRAWS MANGA.

BUT I'M FAR FROM THE ONLY PERSON IN JAPAN...

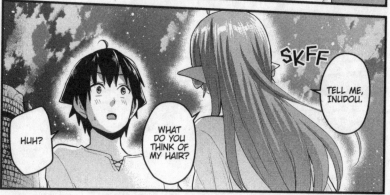

SKFF

HUH?

WHAT DO YOU THINK OF MY HAIR?

TELL ME, INUDOU.

HOW DO YOU FEEL ABOUT ME?
Clench

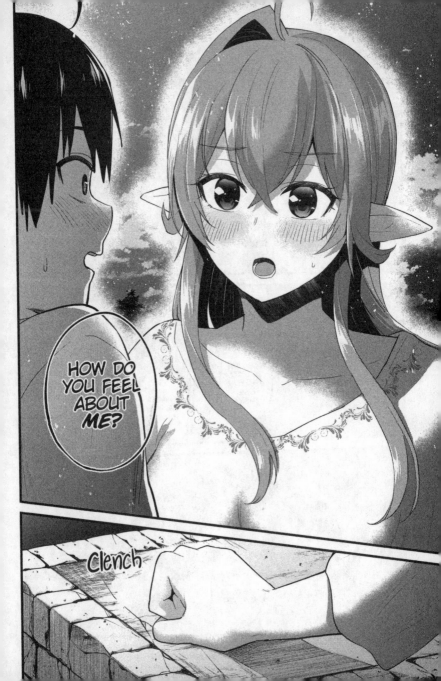

Does a Hot Elf Live NEXT DOOR to You?

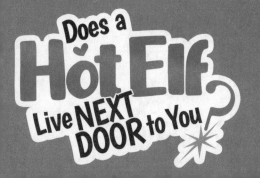

Does a Hot Elf Live NEXT DOOR to You?

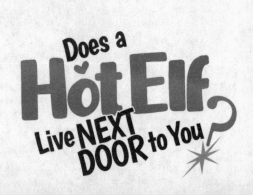

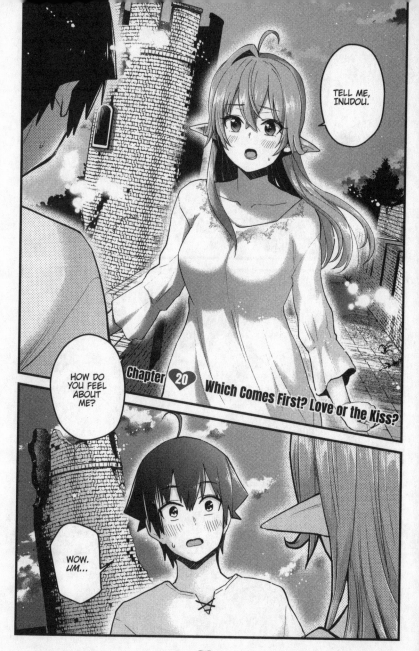

TELL ME, INUDOU.

HOW DO YOU FEEL ABOUT ME?

Chapter **20** Which Comes First? Love or the Kiss?

WOW. UM...

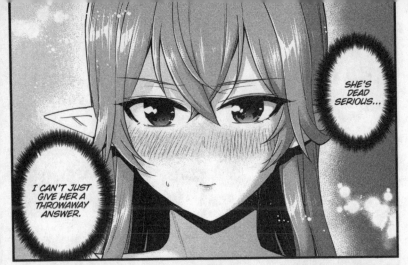

SHE'S DEAD SERIOUS...

I CAN'T JUST GIVE HER A THROWAWAY ANSWER.

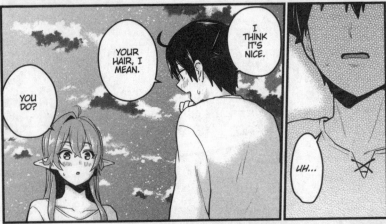

YOU DO?

YOUR HAIR, I MEAN.

I THINK IT'S NICE.

UH...

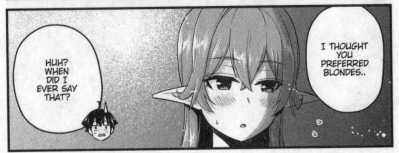

HUH? WHEN DID I EVER SAY THAT?

I THOUGHT YOU PREFERRED BLONDES..

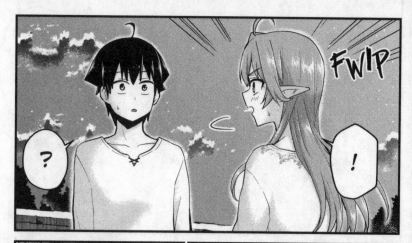

?

!

FWIP

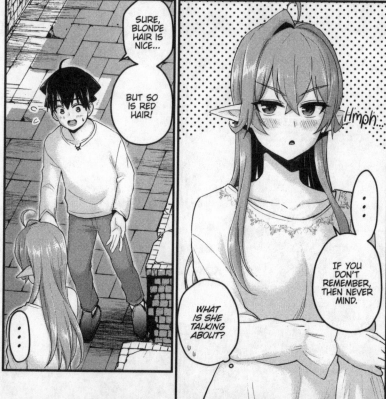

SURE, BLONDE HAIR IS NICE...

BUT SO IS RED HAIR!

Hmph...

...

WHAT IS SHE TALKING ABOUT?

IF YOU DON'T REMEMBER, THEN NEVER MIND.

...

IT'S BEAUTIFUL LIKE THE SUNSET.
IT EVEN SMELLS GOOD.
ANYWAY, I LOVE YOUR HAIR, SURT-SAN!

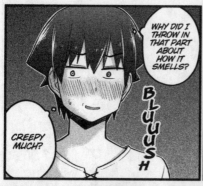

WHY DID I THROW IN THAT PART ABOUT HOW IT SMELLS?

CREEPY MUCH?

BLUUUSH

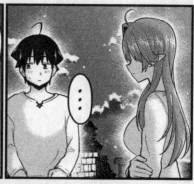

...

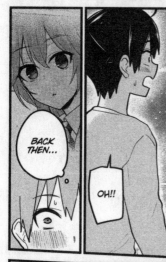

BACK THEN...

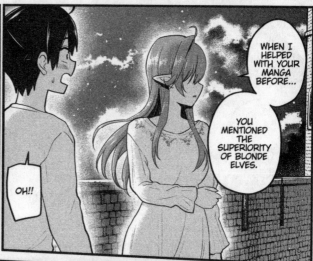

WHEN I HELPED WITH YOUR MANGA BEFORE...

YOU MENTIONED THE SUPERIORITY OF BLONDE ELVES.

OH!!

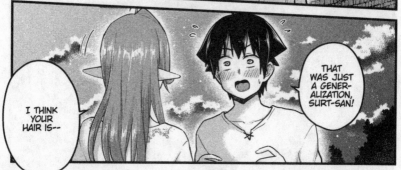

THAT WAS JUST A GENER- ALIZATION, SURT-SAN!

I THINK YOUR HAIR IS--

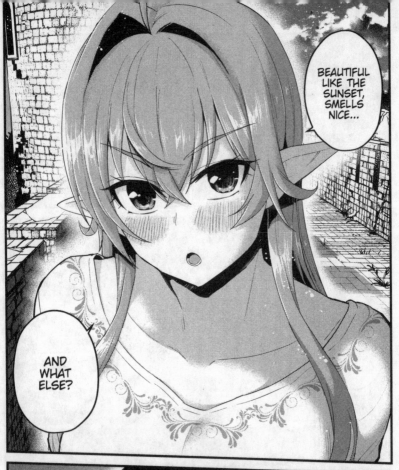

BEAUTIFUL LIKE THE SUNSET, SMELLS NICE...

AND WHAT ELSE?

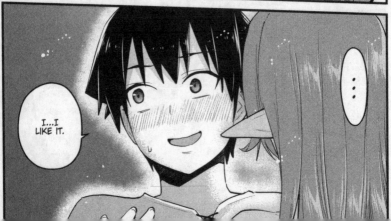

I...I LIKE IT.

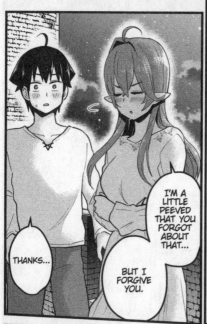

I'M A LITTLE PEEVED THAT YOU FORGOT ABOUT THAT...

THANKS...

BUT I FORGIVE YOU.

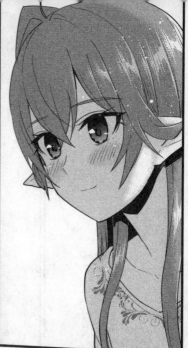

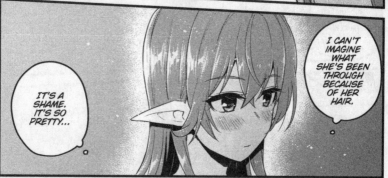

IT'S A SHAME. IT'S SO PRETTY...

I CAN'T IMAGINE WHAT SHE'S BEEN THROUGH BECAUSE OF HER HAIR.

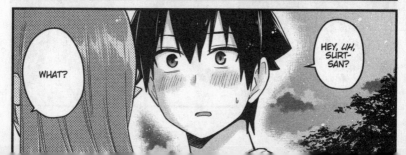

WHAT?

HEY, UH, SURT-SAN?

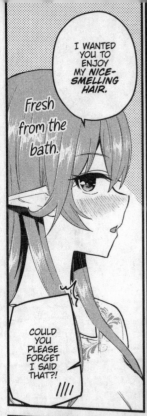

I WANTED YOU TO ENJOY MY *NICE-SMELLING* HAIR.

Fresh from the bath.

COULD YOU PLEASE FORGET I SAID THAT?!

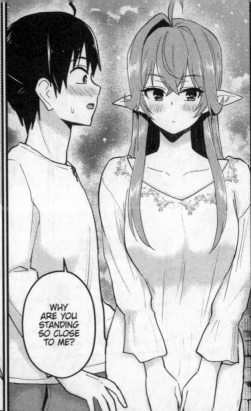

WHY ARE YOU STANDING SO CLOSE TO ME?

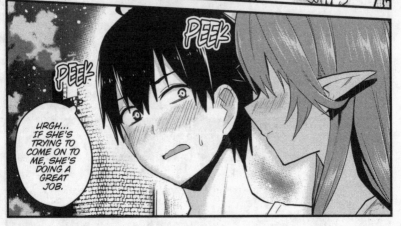

PEEK

PEEK

URGH... IF SHE'S TRYING TO COME ON TO ME, SHE'S DOING A GREAT JOB.

I KNOW SHE'S A HYPER-EXPLOSIVE WALKING DISASTER-SLASH-OTAKU...
BUT ALL I SEE NOW IS A REGULAR, PRETTY GIRL...
INUDOU?
FWAH?! YES? WHAT IS IT?
ABOUT WHAT HAPPENED THIS AFTER-NOON...
FWSH
Naked♥
WHAT DIDN'T HAPPEN?!
THE K...
THE WHAT?

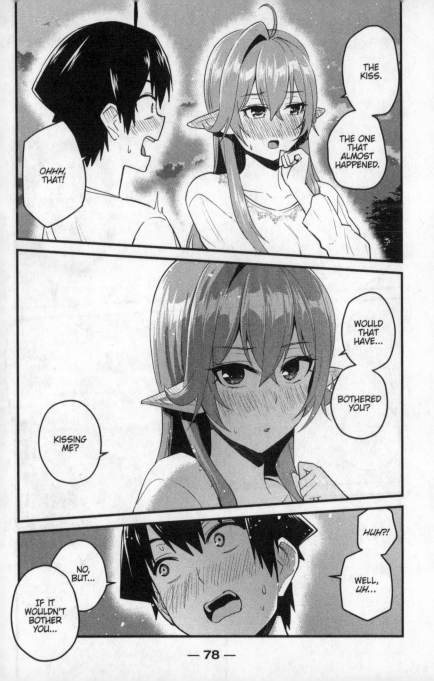

THE KISS.

THE ONE THAT ALMOST HAPPENED.

OHHH, THAT!

WOULD THAT HAVE...

BOTHERED YOU?

KISSING ME?

HUH?!

WELL, UH...

NO, BUT...

IF IT WOULDN'T BOTHER YOU...

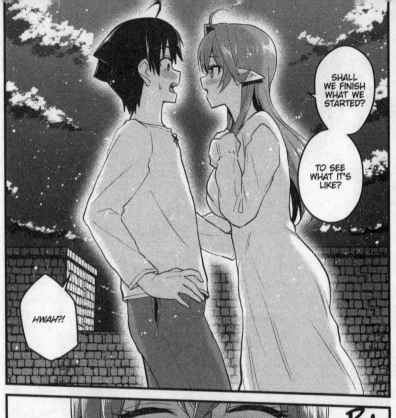

SHALL WE FINISH WHAT WE STARTED?

TO SEE WHAT IT'S LIKE?

HWAH?!

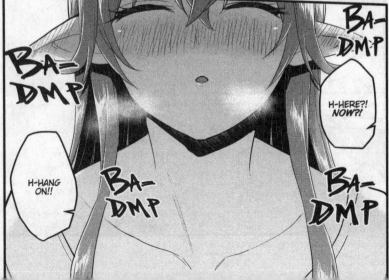

BA-DMP

BA-DMP

H-HERE?! NOW?!

H-HANG ON!!

BA-DMP

BA-DMP

YOU SHOULD ONLY KISS SOMEONE YOU LO--
UGOH??!
BZZZZZZ
BZZZ
WHAT THE HECK?! GIANT DRONE BEETLES?!
BZZZ
SPIRIT INSECTS?! OH, DON'T TELL ME...!
BZZZ
SKSH
SKSH
UNHAND ME, FAFNIR! I WILL NOT BE DENIED MY RIGHT!
WHUD

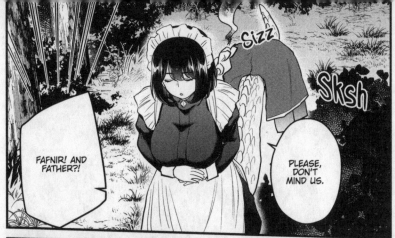

FAFNIR! AND FATHER?!

PLEASE, DON'T MIND US.

Sizz

Sksh

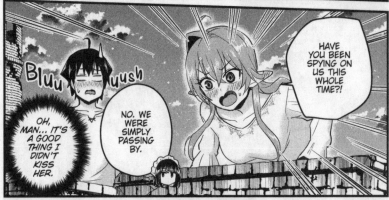

HAVE YOU BEEN SPYING ON US THIS WHOLE TIME?!

OH, MAN... IT'S A GOOD THING I DIDN'T KISS HER.

NO. WE WERE SIMPLY PASSING BY.

Bluuuush

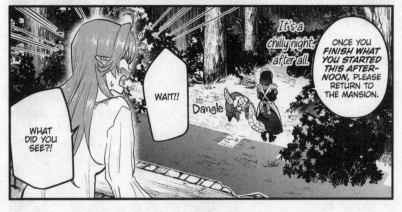

ONCE YOU *FINISH WHAT YOU STARTED* THIS AFTERNOON, PLEASE RETURN TO THE MANSION.

It's a chilly night, after all.

WAIT!!

Dangle

WHAT DID YOU SEE?!

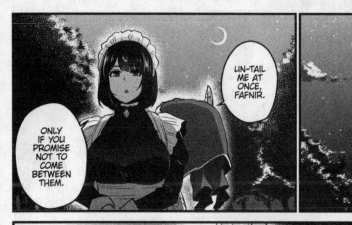

UN-TAIL ME AT ONCE, FAFNIR.

ONLY IF YOU PROMISE NOT TO COME BETWEEN THEM.

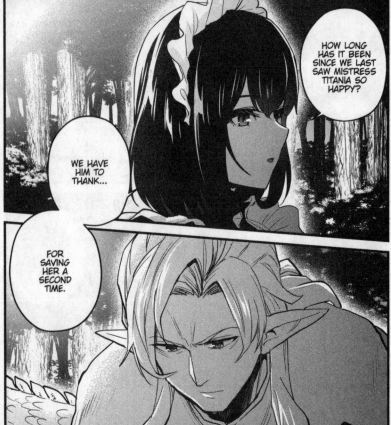

HOW LONG HAS IT BEEN SINCE WE LAST SAW MISTRESS TITANIA SO HAPPY?

WE HAVE HIM TO THANK...

FOR SAVING HER A SECOND TIME.

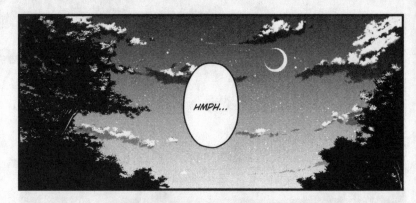

HMPH...

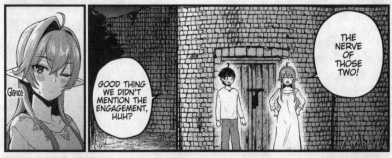

Glance

GOOD THING WE DIDN'T MENTION THE ENGAGEMENT, HUH?

THE NERVE OF THOSE TWO!

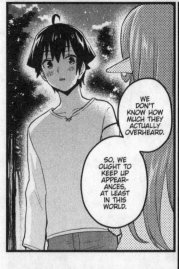

WE DON'T KNOW HOW MUCH THEY ACTUALLY OVERHEARD.

SO, WE OUGHT TO KEEP UP APPEARANCES, AT LEAST IN THIS WORLD.

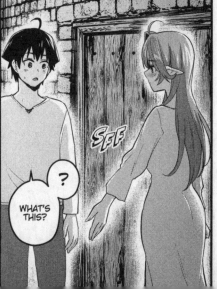

SFF

?

WHAT'S THIS?

OR DO YOU BELIEVE...
ONE MUSTN'T HOLD HANDS UNLESS ONE IS IN LOVE, EITHER?

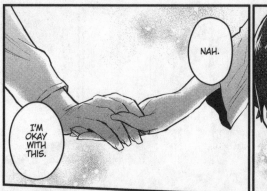

NAH.

I'M OKAY WITH THIS.

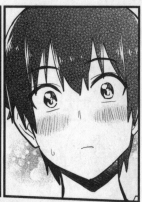

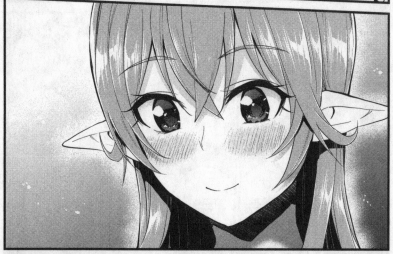

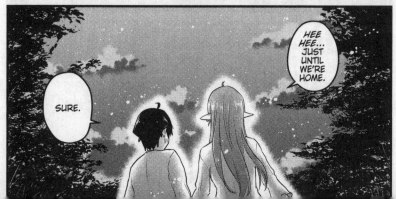

HEE HEE... JUST UNTIL WE'RE HOME.

SURE.

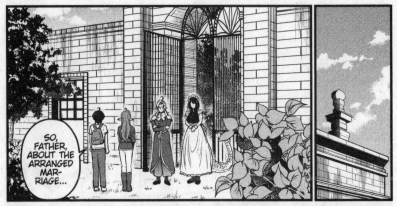

SO, FATHER, ABOUT THE ARRANGED MARRIAGE...

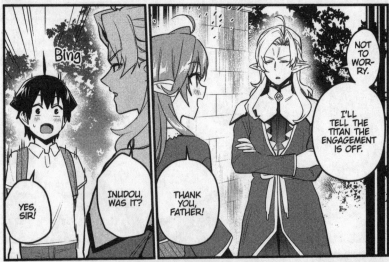

Bing

YES, SIR!

INUDOU, WAS IT?

THANK YOU, FATHER!

NOT TO WORRY.

I'LL TELL THE TITAN THE ENGAGEMENT IS OFF.

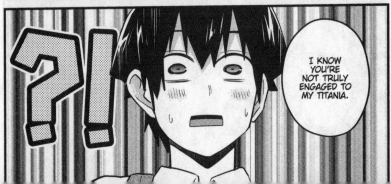

?!

I KNOW YOU'RE NOT TRULY ENGAGED TO MY TITANIA.

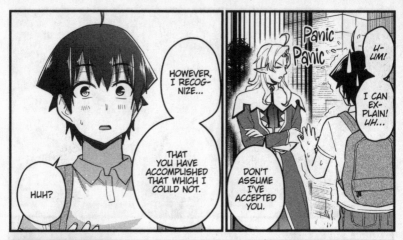

HOWEVER, I RECOG-NIZE...

THAT YOU HAVE ACCOMPLISHED THAT WHICH I COULD NOT.

HUH?

Panic Panic

U-UM!

I CAN EX-PLAIN! UH...

DON'T ASSUME I'VE ACCEPTED YOU.

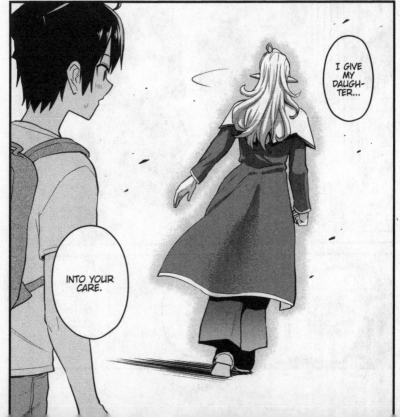

I GIVE MY DAUGH-TER...

INTO YOUR CARE.

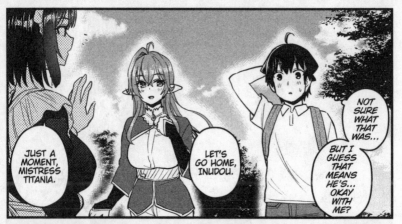

JUST A MOMENT, MISTRESS TITANIA.

LET'S GO HOME, INUDOU.

NOT SURE WHAT THAT WAS...

BUT I GUESS THAT MEANS HE'S... OKAY WITH ME?

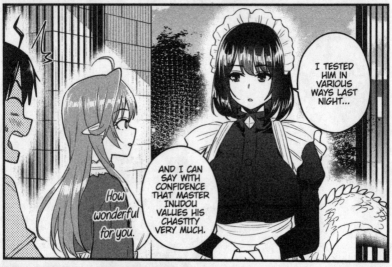

I TESTED HIM IN VARIOUS WAYS LAST NIGHT...

AND I CAN SAY WITH CONFIDENCE THAT MASTER INUDOU VALUES HIS CHASTITY VERY MUCH.

How wonderful for you.

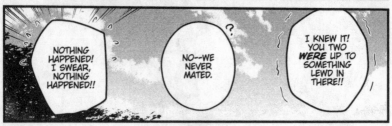

NOTHING HAPPENED! I SWEAR, NOTHING HAPPENED!!

NO--WE NEVER MATED.

I KNEW IT! YOU TWO *WERE* UP TO SOMETHING LEWD IN THERE!!

Does a Hot Elf Live NEXT DOOR to You?

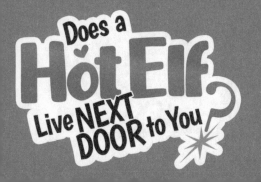

Does a Hot Elf Live NEXT DOOR to You?

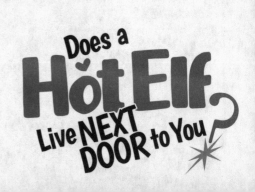

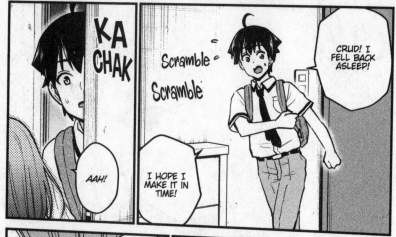

KA CHAK

Scramble

Scramble

AAH!

I HOPE I MAKE IT IN TIME!

CRUD! I FELL BACK ASLEEP!

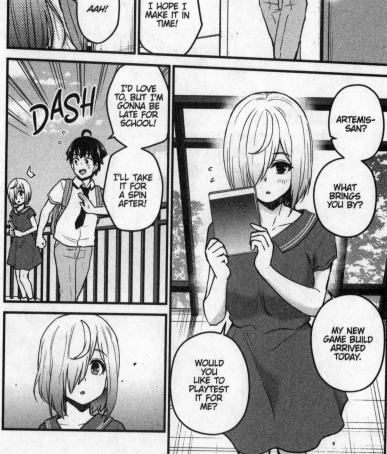

DASH

I'D LOVE TO, BUT I'M GONNA BE LATE FOR SCHOOL!

I'LL TAKE IT FOR A SPIN AFTER!

ARTEMIS-SAN?

WHAT BRINGS YOU BY?

MY NEW GAME BUILD ARRIVED TODAY.

WOULD YOU LIKE TO PLAYTEST IT FOR ME?

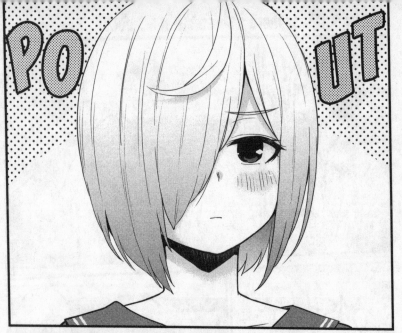

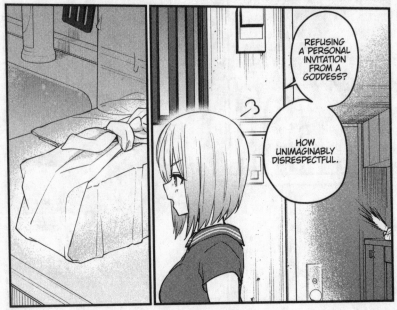

REFUSING A PERSONAL INVITATION FROM A GODDESS?

HOW UNIMAGINABLY DISRESPECTFUL.

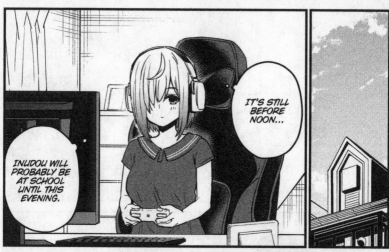

IT'S STILL BEFORE NOON...

INUDOU WILL PROBABLY BE AT SCHOOL UNTIL THIS EVENING.

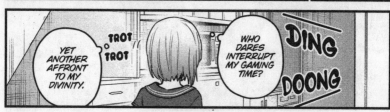

YET ANOTHER AFFRONT TO MY DIVINITY.

TROT TROT

WHO DARES INTERRUPT MY GAMING TIME?

DING DOONG

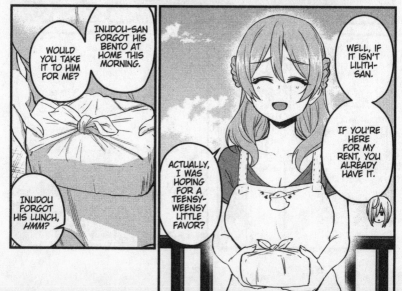

INUDOU-SAN FORGOT HIS BENTO AT HOME THIS MORNING.

WOULD YOU TAKE IT TO HIM FOR ME?

INUDOU FORGOT HIS LUNCH, HMM?

WELL, IF IT ISN'T LILITH-SAN.

IF YOU'RE HERE FOR MY RENT, YOU ALREADY HAVE IT.

ACTUALLY, I WAS HOPING FOR A TEENSY-WEENSY LITTLE FAVOR?

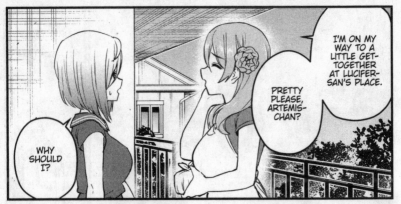

I'M ON MY WAY TO A LITTLE GET-TOGETHER AT LUCIFER-SAN'S PLACE.

PRETTY PLEASE, ARTEMIS-CHAN?

WHY SHOULD I?

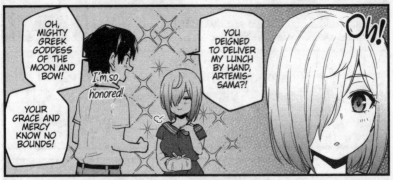

OH, MIGHTY GREEK GODDESS OF THE MOON AND BOW!

YOUR GRACE AND MERCY KNOW NO BOUNDS!

I'm so honored!

YOU DEIGNED TO DELIVER MY LUNCH BY HAND, ARTEMIS-SAMA?!

Oh!

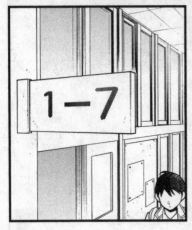

1—7

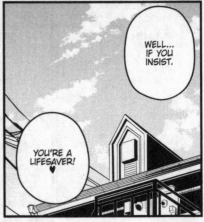

WELL... IF YOU INSIST.

YOU'RE A LIFESAVER! ♥

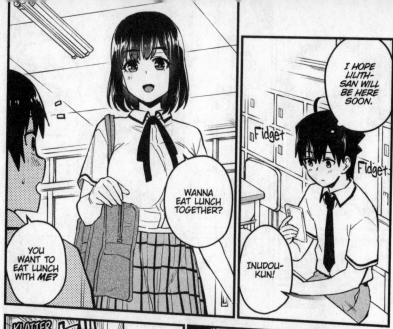

I HOPE LILITH-SAN WILL BE HERE SOON.

WANNA EAT LUNCH TOGETHER?

YOU WANT TO EAT LUNCH WITH *ME*?

Fidget

Fidget

INUDOU-KUN!

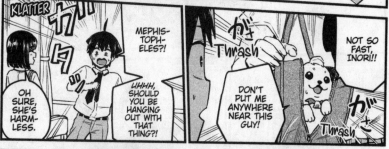

KLATTER

MEPHISTOPH-ELES?!

UHHH, SHOULD YOU BE HANGING OUT WITH THAT THING?!

OH SURE, SHE'S HARMLESS.

Thrash

NOT SO FAST, INORI!!

DON'T PUT ME ANYWHERE NEAR THIS GUY!

Thrash

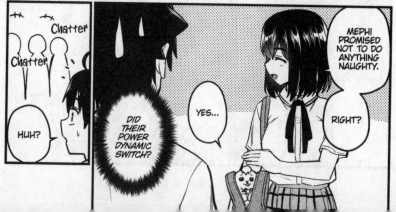

Chatter

Chatter

MEPHI PROMISED NOT TO DO ANYTHING NAUGHTY.

YES...

RIGHT?

HUH?

DID THEIR POWER DYNAMIC SWITCH?

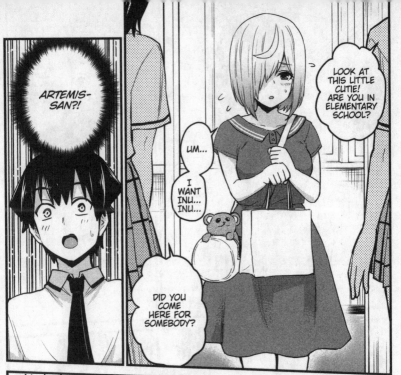

ARTEMIS-SAN?!

LOOK AT THIS LITTLE CUTIE! ARE YOU IN ELEMENTARY SCHOOL?

UM...

I WANT INU... INU...

DID YOU COME HERE FOR SOMEBODY?

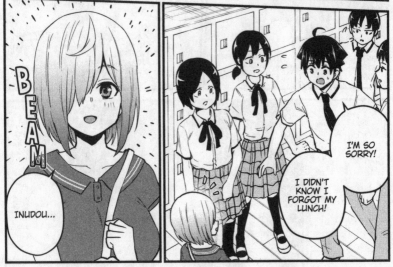

BEAM

INUDOU...

I'M SO SORRY!

I DIDN'T KNOW I FORGOT MY LUNCH!

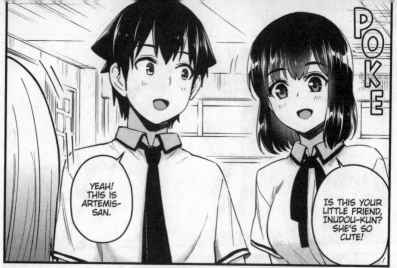

POKE

YEAH! THIS IS ARTEMIS-SAN.

IS THIS YOUR LITTLE FRIEND, INUDOU-KUN? SHE'S SO CUTE!

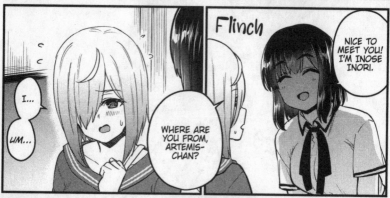

Flinch

I...

UM...

WHERE ARE YOU FROM, ARTEMIS-CHAN?

NICE TO MEET YOU! I'M INOSE INORI.

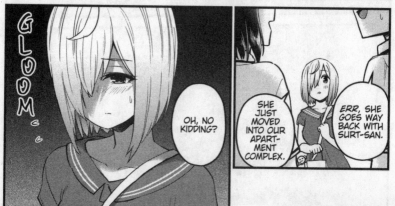

GLOOM

OH, NO KIDDING?

SHE JUST MOVED INTO OUR APART-MENT COMPLEX.

ERR, SHE GOES WAY BACK WITH SURT-SAN.

IT'S SUCH A BEAUTIFUL DAY. WE SHOULD EAT OUTSIDE!
WHOA!
Squeeze

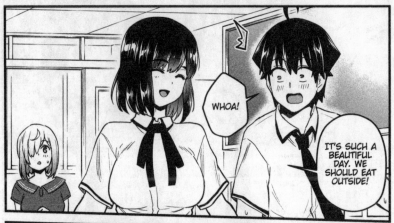

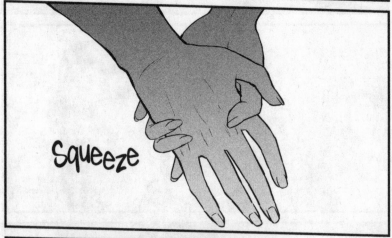

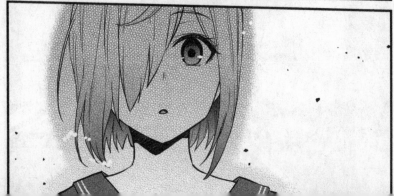

WHY DON'T YOU COME WITH US, ARTEMIS-CHA--
FLASH
Wish Upon the Moon:
Moonlight Rhapsody

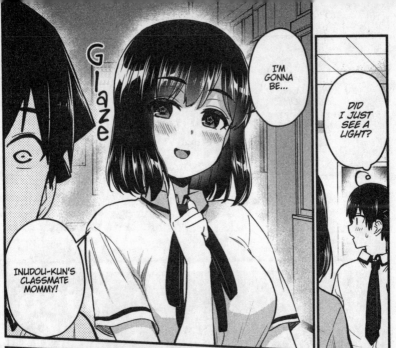

I'M GONNA BE...

DID I JUST SEE A LIGHT?

INUDOU-KUN'S CLASSMATE MOMMY!

Glaze

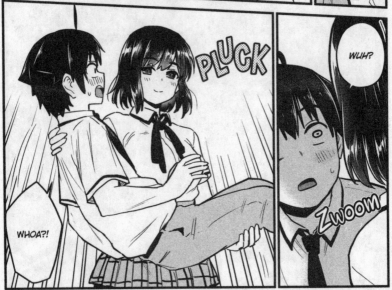

PLUCK

WHOA?!

WUH?

Zwoom

WHAT A BIG WIDDLE BABY!
DOES WIDDLE BABY HAVE BIG HUNGIE?
?!
WH-WH-WHAT'S GOTTEN INTO YOU?!
TIME FOR MILKY-WILKY!
Pop
WHAT THE--?!
Pop

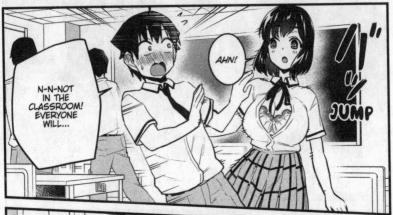

AHN!

N-N-NOT IN THE CLASSROOM! EVERYONE WILL...

JUMP

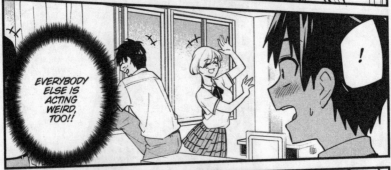

EVERYBODY ELSE IS ACTING WEIRD, TOO!!

!

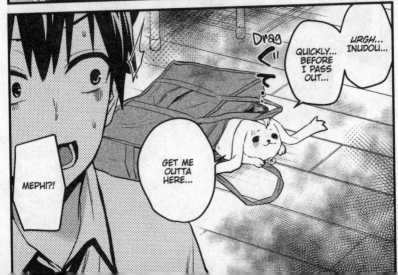

Drag

URGH... INUDOU...

QUICKLY... BEFORE I PASS OUT...

MEPHI?!

GET ME OUTTA HERE...

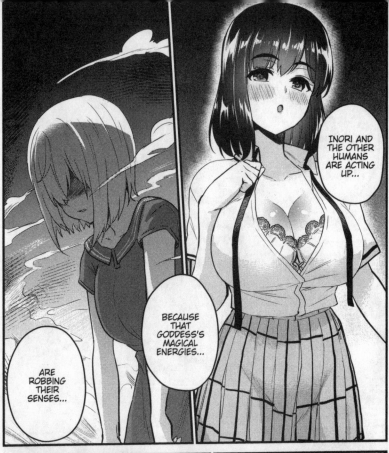

INORI AND THE OTHER HUMANS ARE ACTING UP...

BECAUSE THAT GODDESS'S MAGICAL ENERGIES...

ARE ROBBING THEIR SENSES...

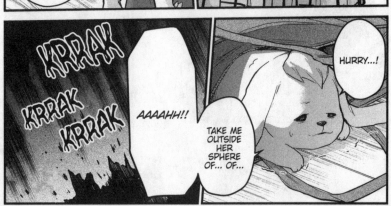

KRRAK

KRRAK KRRAK

AAAAHH!!

TAKE ME OUTSIDE HER SPHERE OF... OF...

HURRY...!

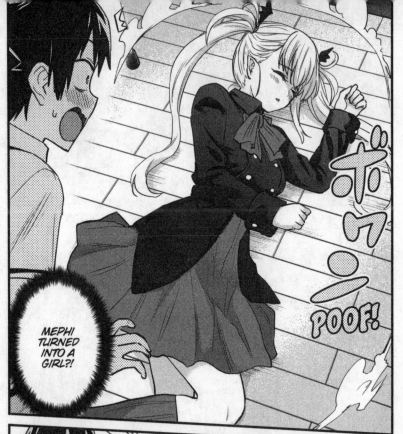

POOF!

MEPHI TURNED INTO A GIRL?!

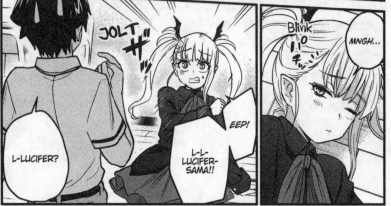

JOLT

MNGH...

Blink

L-LUCIFER?

EEP!

L-L-LUCIFER-SAMA!!

I'M SORRY! I'M SO, SO SORRY!
ぬぎ
Strip
ぬぎっ
Strip
I'LL FILL MY QUOTA NEXT TIME, I SWEAR!
WHOA!!
Hide
STOP THAT!!
KER-GROVEL
土下座ァアン
PLEASE GIVE ME A PASS, JUST THIS ONCE!
WHAT THE HELL IS THIS DEMON DOING?!
I HAVE A DYING MOTHER AT HOME!!
WHATEVER! JUST GET DRESSED!!

Juicy ♥
PLEASE DON'T FIRE ME! I NEED THIS JOB!!
Juicy ♥
YOUR MOMMY...
WILL TAKE VEWWY, VEWWY GOOD CARE OF CWASSMATE BABY, YES SHE WILL!
HUMMA HUMMA

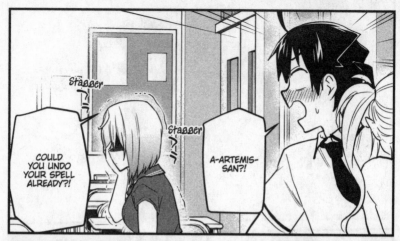

stagger

stagger

?!

COULD YOU UNDO YOUR SPELL ALREADY?!

A-ARTEMIS-SAN?!

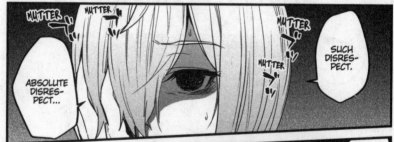

MUTTER

MUTTER

MUTTER

MUTTER

ABSOLUTE DISRES-PECT...

SUCH DISRES-PECT.

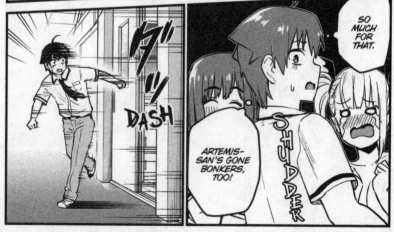

DASH

SO MUCH FOR THAT.

ARTEMIS-SAN'S GONE BONKERS, TOO!

SHUDDER

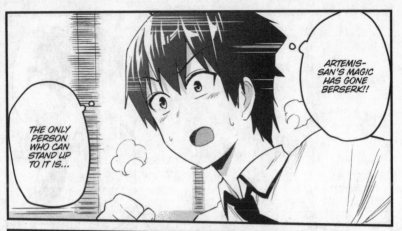

ARTEMIS-SAN'S MAGIC HAS GONE BERSERK!!

THE ONLY PERSON WHO CAN STAND UP TO IT IS...

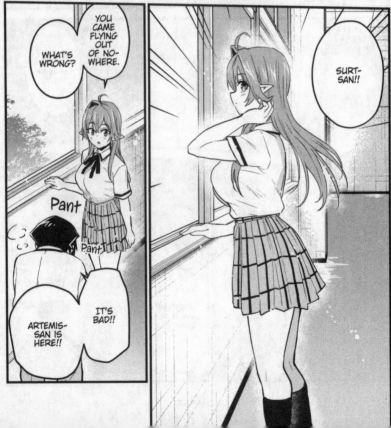

YOU CAME FLYING OUT OF NOWHERE.

WHAT'S WRONG?

SURT-SAN!!

Pant

Pant

IT'S BAD!!

ARTEMIS-SAN IS HERE!!

OH, IS SHE NOW? WELL, FANCY THAT.
THERE'S NOTHING FANCY ABOUT IT!!
HER MAGIC'S GONE TOTALLY BERSERK!!
EVERYONE'S LOSING THEIR MINDS!
YOU'RE THE ONLY PERSON WHO CAN HELP HER!
I SEE...
IF I FIX THIS FOR YOU...
SLIP
HUH?

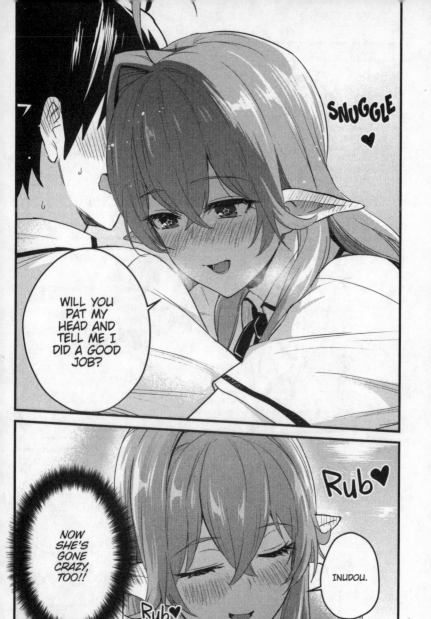

SNUGGLE ♥

WILL YOU PAT MY HEAD AND TELL ME I DID A GOOD JOB?

Rub ♥

NOW SHE'S GONE CRAZY, TOO!!

INUDOU.

Rub ♥

Does a Hot Elf Live NEXT DOOR to You?

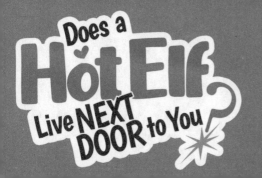

Does a Hot Elf Live NEXT DOOR to You?

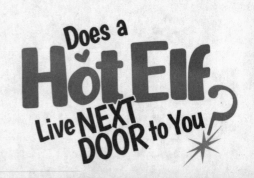

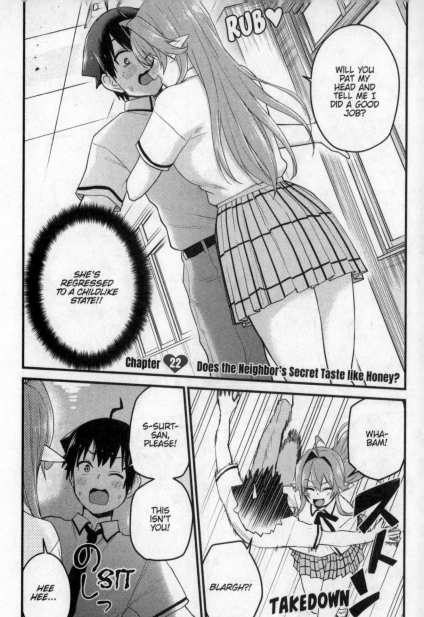

RUB ♡

WILL YOU PAT MY HEAD AND TELL ME I DID A GOOD JOB?

SHE'S REGRESSED TO A CHILDLIKE STATE!!

Chapter 22 Does the Neighbor's Secret Taste like Honey?

S-SURT-SAN, PLEASE!

THIS ISN'T YOU!

HEE HEE...

SIT

WHA-BAM!

BLARGH?!

TAKEDOWN

— 113 —

INUDOU.
I LOVE YOU.
BA-DMP
HUH?!
SHOVE
NO!
SHE ISN'T HERSELF RIGHT NOW!
SNAP OUT OF IT, PLEASE...!

DIS-RESPECT.
Shiing
ARTEMIS-SAN!
GRIKK
DIS-RESPECT.
GRIKK
GRIKK
IS THAT... AN ATTACK SPELL?
OH GAWD! NO, NO, NO!!
SHOOM

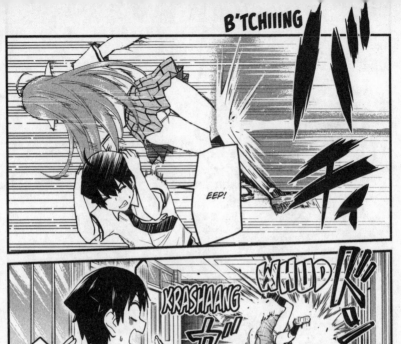

B'TCHIIIING

EEP!

KRASHAANG

WHUD

SURT-SAN!!
ARE YOU
OKAY?!

KRANK

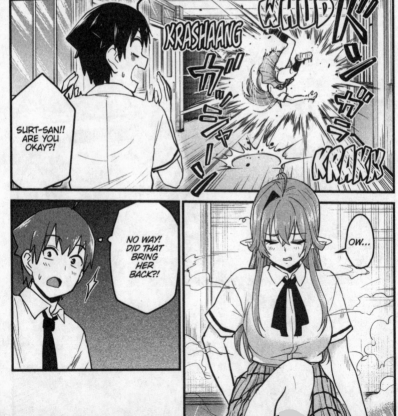

NO WAY!
DID THAT
BRING
HER
BACK?!

OW...

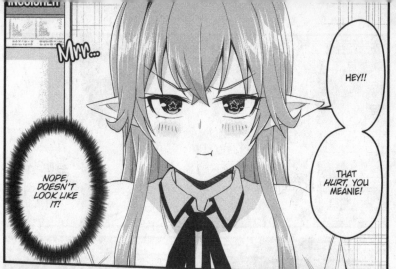

HEY!!

THAT *HURT*, YOU MEANIE!

NOPE, DOESN'T LOOK LIKE IT!

Mmm...

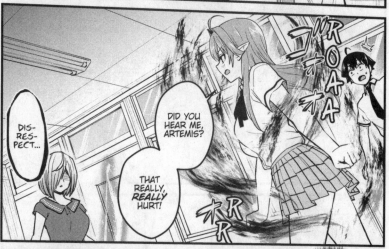

DIS-RES-PECT...

DID YOU HEAR ME, ARTEMIS?

THAT REALLY, *REALLY* HURT!

ROAA

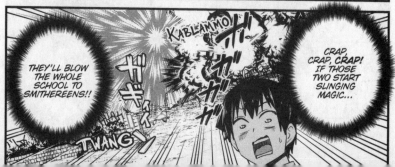

THEY'LL BLOW THE WHOLE SCHOOL TO SMITHEREENS!!

CRAP, CRAP, CRAP! IF THOSE TWO START SLINGING MAGIC...

KABLAMMO

TWANG

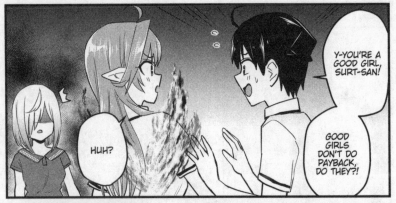

HUH?

Y-YOU'RE A GOOD GIRL, SURT-SAN!

GOOD GIRLS DON'T DO PAYBACK, DO THEY?!

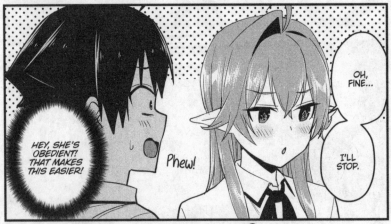

HEY, SHE'S OBEDIENT! THAT MAKES THIS EASIER!

Phew!

OH, FINE...

I'LL STOP.

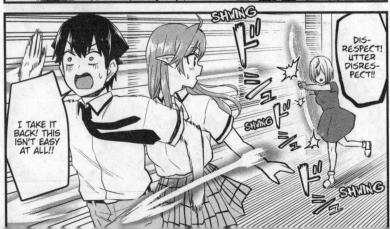

I TAKE IT BACK! THIS ISN'T EASY AT ALL!!

SHMING

SHMING

SHMING

DIS-RESPECT! UTTER DISRESPECT!!

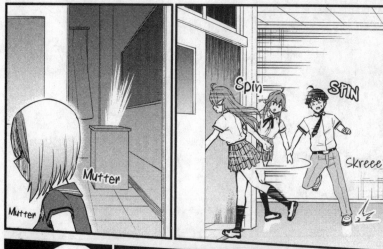

Mutter

Mutter

Spin

Spin

Skreee

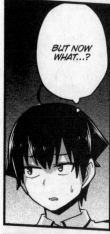

BUT NOW WHAT...?

I THINK WE LOST HER...

Giddy

Giddy

Ba-dmp

Ba-dmp

SQUEEZE

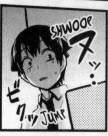

SHWOOP

JUMP

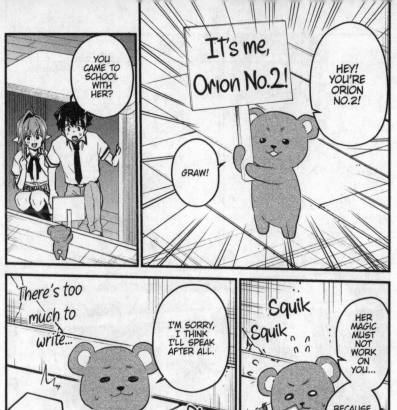

YOU CAME TO SCHOOL WITH HER?

It's me, Orion No.2!

HEY! YOU'RE ORION NO.2!

GRAW!

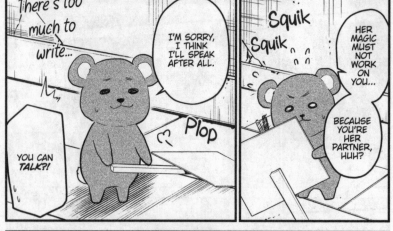

There's too much to write...

I'M SORRY, I THINK I'LL SPEAK AFTER ALL.

YOU CAN *TALK*?!

Plop

Squik

Squik

HER MAGIC MUST NOT WORK ON YOU...

BECAUSE YOU'RE HER PARTNER, HUH?

Dad

Raw!

THAT'D BE A SHOCKER, ALL RIGHT...

Don't forget: I'm a divine beast!

I DIDN'T WISH TO SCARE YOU WITH MY MIND-SPEECH.

INUDOU-SAN, YOU CAUSED THIS MAGICAL MAYHEM.
THUS, ONLY YOU CAN PUT A STOP TO IT.
WHO, ME?!
THIS IS ALSO WHY YOU ARE IMMUNE TO ITS EFFECTS.
MOONLIGHT RHAPSODY...
IS A SPELL THAT DESTROYS THE INHIBITIONS OF ANYONE WITHIN ITS RADIUS.
FOR SOME, THIS REVEALS THEIR INGRAINED HABITS.
FOR OTHERS, IT REVEALS THEIR SECRET, INNERMOST DESIRES...
Time for milky-wilky!
ONCE THE SPELL IS ACTIVATED, NOT EVEN ARTEMIS-SAMA HERSELF CAN CONTROL IT.
Pop

FOR NOW, ITS EFFECTS ARE RESTRICTED TO WITHIN THE SCHOOL WALLS...
BUT LEFT UNCHECKED, IT WILL SOON OVERTAKE THE ENTIRE CITY.
YOU GOTTA BE KIDDING ME...
AND YOU'RE SAYING...
I HAVE TO FIX THIS? *HOW?!*
MOONLIGHT RHAPSODY ONLY ACTIVATES...
WHEN ARTEMIS-SAMA'S UNHAPPINESS EXPLODES.

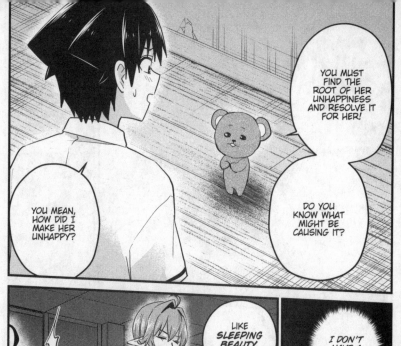

YOU MUST FIND THE ROOT OF HER UNHAPPINESS AND RESOLVE IT FOR HER!

DO YOU KNOW WHAT MIGHT BE CAUSING IT?

YOU MEAN, HOW DID I MAKE HER UNHAPPY?

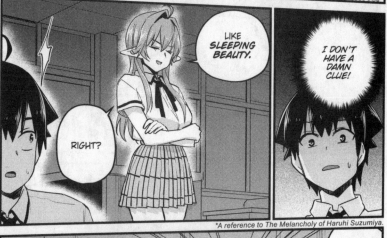

LIKE SLEEPING BEAUTY.

RIGHT?

I DON'T HAVE A DAMN CLUE!

*A reference to The Melancholy of Haruhi Suzumiya.

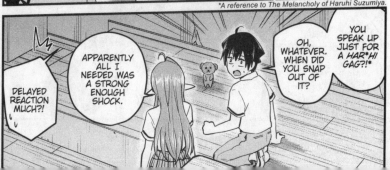

YOU SPEAK UP JUST FOR A HAR*HI GAG?!*

OH, WHATEVER. WHEN DID YOU SNAP OUT OF IT?

APPARENTLY ALL I NEEDED WAS A STRONG ENOUGH SHOCK.

DELAYED REACTION MUCH?!

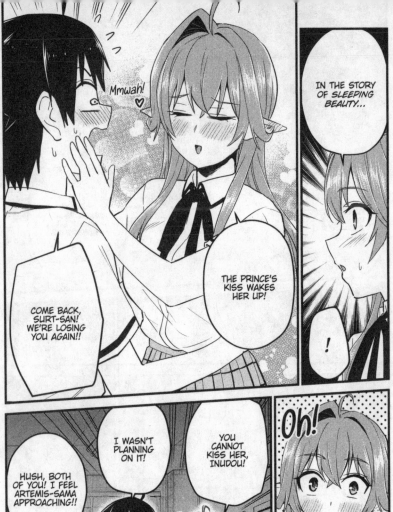

Mmwah! ♥

IN THE STORY OF *SLEEPING BEAUTY*...

THE PRINCE'S KISS WAKES HER UP!

COME BACK, SURT-SAN! WE'RE LOSING YOU AGAIN!!

!

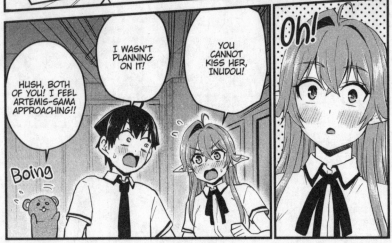

HUSH, BOTH OF YOU! I FEEL ARTEMIS-SAMA APPROACHING!!

I WASN'T PLANNING ON IT!

YOU CANNOT KISS HER, INUDOU!

Oh!

Boing

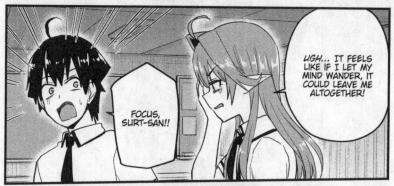

UGH... IT FEELS LIKE IF I LET MY MIND WANDER, IT COULD LEAVE ME ALTOGETHER!

FOCUS, SURT-SAN!!

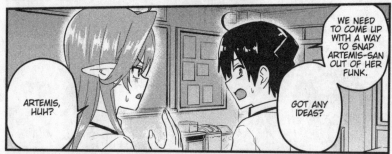

ARTEMIS, HUH?

WE NEED TO COME UP WITH A WAY TO SNAP ARTEMIS-SAN OUT OF HER FUNK.

GOT ANY IDEAS?

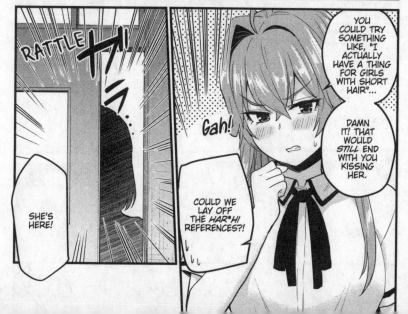

RATTLE

...!

YOU COULD TRY SOMETHING LIKE, "I ACTUALLY HAVE A THING FOR GIRLS WITH SHORT HAIR"...

DAMN IT! THAT WOULD *STILL* END WITH YOU KISSING HER.

Gah!

COULD WE LAY OFF THE *HAR*HI REFERENCES?!

SHE'S HERE!

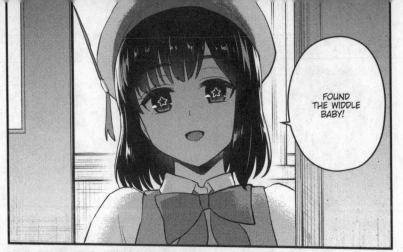

FOUND THE WIDDLE BABY!

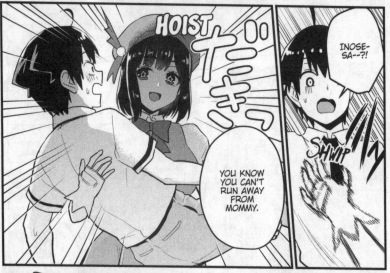

HOIST

INOSE-SA--?!

YOU KNOW YOU CAN'T RUN AWAY FROM MOMMY.

SHWIP

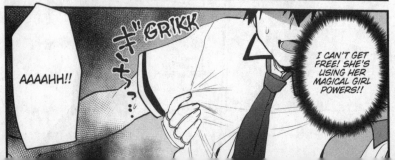

GRIKK

AAAAHH!!

I CAN'T GET FREE! SHE'S USING HER MAGICAL GIRL POWERS!!

INORI!!
WHAT ARE YOU DOING TO LUCIFER-SAMA?!
NUDE
WOULD YOU PUT SOME CLOTHES ON?!
Aagh!
Aagh!
Sway
ゆら…
Gleam
DISRESPECT...
YOU'RE IN DANGER, INUDOU-SAN!!
TELL ME SOMETHING I DON'T KNOW!!
GRIKK
ギリ
GRIKK
ギリ
GRIKK
ギリ
STEP AWAY FROM THE WOMEN.

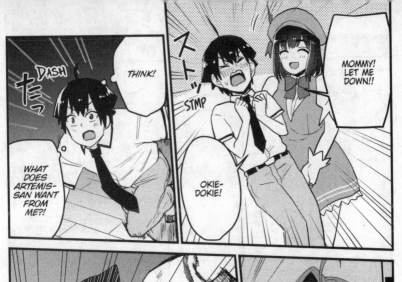

THINK!

DASH

WHAT DOES ARTEMIS-SAN WANT FROM ME?!

STMP

OKIE-DOKIE!

MOMMY! LET ME DOWN!!

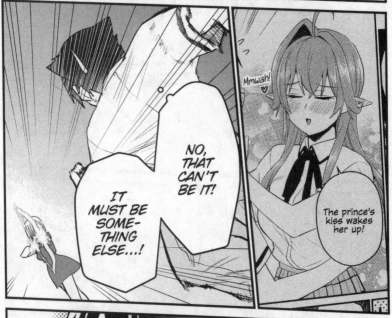

NO, THAT CAN'T BE IT!

IT MUST BE SOME-THING ELSE...!

Mmwah!

The prince's kiss wakes her up!

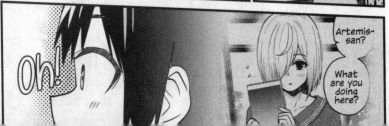

Oh!

Artemis-san?

What are you doing here?

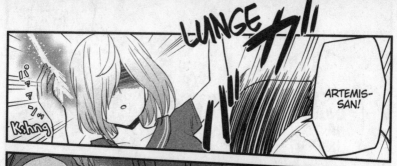

LUNGE

ARTEMIS-SAN!

Kshng

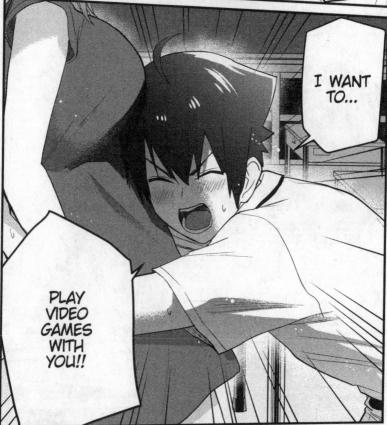

I WANT TO...

PLAY VIDEO GAMES WITH YOU!!

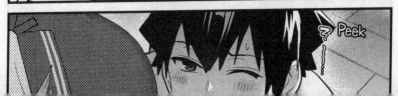

Peek

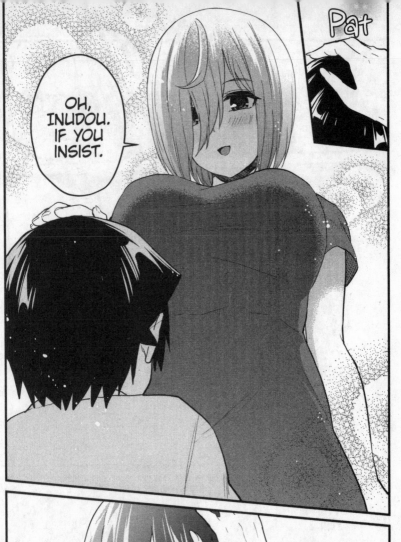

Pat

OH, INUDOU. IF YOU INSIST.

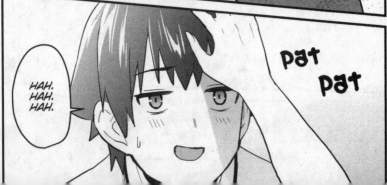

HAH. HAH. HAH.

Pat Pat

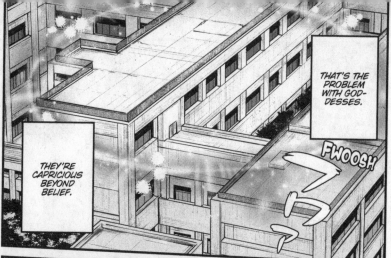

THAT'S THE PROBLEM WITH GODDESSES.

THEY'RE CAPRICIOUS BEYOND BELIEF.

FWOOSH

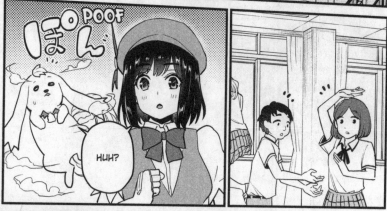

POOF

HUH?

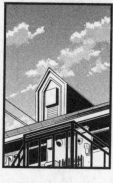

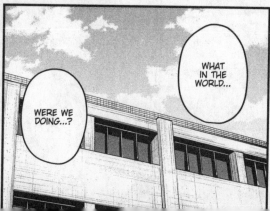

WHAT IN THE WORLD...

WERE WE DOING...?

For, others, it reveals their secret, innermost desires...

NOW THAT I HAVE TIME TO THINK ABOUT IT...

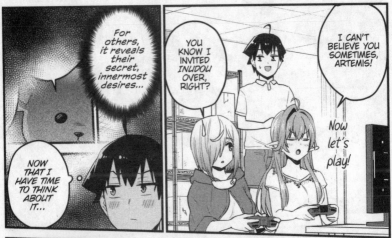

YOU KNOW I INVITED INUIDOU OVER, RIGHT?

I CAN'T BELIEVE YOU SOMETIMES, ARTEMIS!

Now let's play!

ARGH! WHY AM I THE ONLY ONE WHO REMEMBERS ANYTHING?!

This is so annoying!

Z Z Z

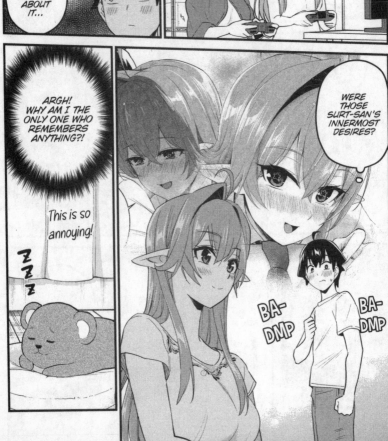

WERE THOSE SURT-SAN'S INNERMOST DESIRES?

BA-DMP

BA-DMP

Does a Hot Elf Live NEXT DOOR to You?

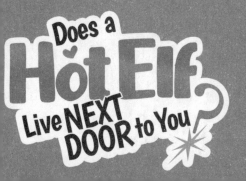

Does a Hot Elf Live NEXT DOOR to You?

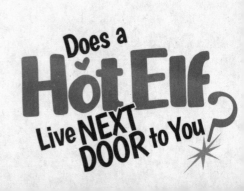

Chapter 23 ❤ Should We Blame It All on Summer?

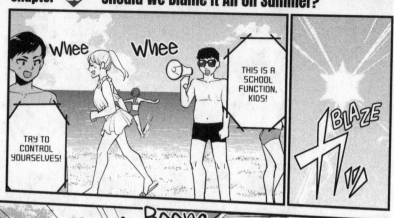

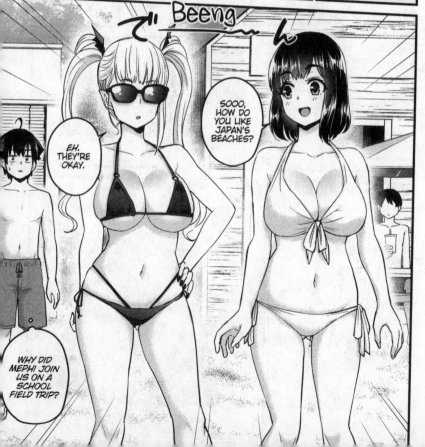

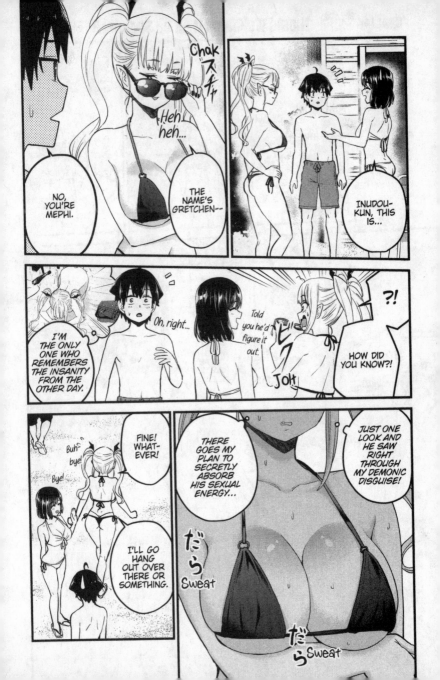

Chak

Heh heh...

NO, YOU'RE MEPHI.

THE NAME'S GRETCHEN--

INUDOU-KUN, THIS IS...

I'M THE ONLY ONE WHO REMEMBERS THE INSANITY FROM THE OTHER DAY.

Oh, right...

Told you he'd figure it out.

Jolt

?!

HOW DID YOU KNOW?!

Buh-bye!

Bye!

FINE! WHAT-EVER!

I'LL GO HANG OUT OVER THERE OR SOMETHING.

THERE GOES MY PLAN TO SECRETLY ABSORB HIS SEXUAL ENERGY...

だら *Sweat*

JUST ONE LOOK AND HE SAW RIGHT THROUGH MY DEMONIC DISGUISE!

だら *Sweat*

WOW. INOSE-SAN IS DOWNRIGHT BLINDING IN THAT SWIMSUIT.
I CAN'T LOOK DIRECTLY AT HER!
Well, maybe a little peek.
Sksh
INUDOU!
Jump
HAVE MERCY! WITH SURT-SAN ADDED TO THIS VISUAL FEAST...
Peek
I'LL HAVE EVEN MORE TROUBLE POLICING MY EYES!!

I FOUND A GRILLED SQUID STAND!
Ah ha ha ha ha!
SURT
Boing
Boing
OH, COME ON!
WHAT ARE YOU WEARING?!
Our school doesn't issue swimsuits!
I SHOULD THINK IT'S OBVIOUS!

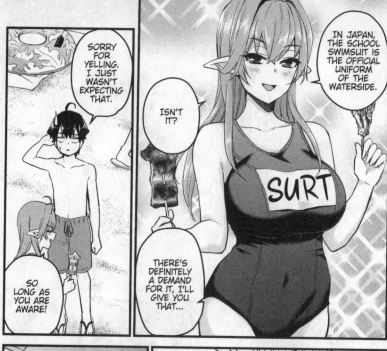

IN JAPAN, THE SCHOOL SWIMSUIT IS THE OFFICIAL UNIFORM OF THE WATERSIDE.

SORRY FOR YELLING. I JUST WASN'T EXPECTING THAT.

ISN'T IT?

SURT

THERE'S DEFINITELY A DEMAND FOR IT, I'LL GIVE YOU THAT...

SO LONG AS YOU ARE AWARE!

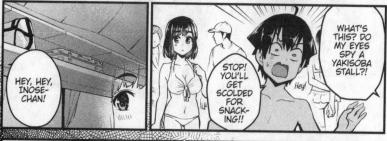

HEY, HEY, INOSE-CHAN!

STOP! YOU'LL GET SCOLDED FOR SNACKING!!

WHAT'S THIS? DO MY EYES SPY A YAKISOBA STALL?!

Hey!

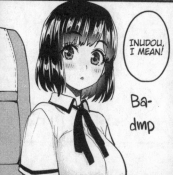

INUDOU, I MEAN!

Ba-dmp

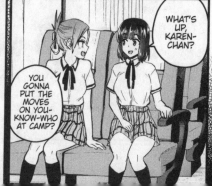

WHAT'S UP, KAREN-CHAN?

YOU GONNA PUT THE MOVES ON YOU-KNOW-WHO AT CAMP?

YOU SHOULD ATTACK HIM IN THAT BIKINI OF YOURS!
WHAT? NO WAY.
THAT'S SO NOT ME.
...
JEEZ. SHE'S A LOST CAUSE.
You should attack him in that bikini of yours!
...
Grab
...
COME HERE FOR A SECOND.
Drag
Drag
HUH?!
WHAT? WHERE ARE WE GOING?

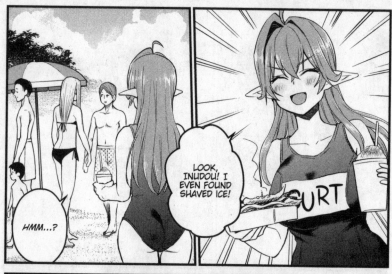

LOOK, INUDOU! I EVEN FOUND SHAVED ICE!

HMM...?

CURT

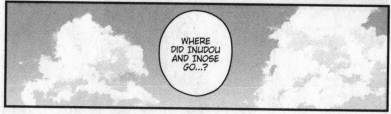

WHERE DID INUDOU AND INOSE GO...?

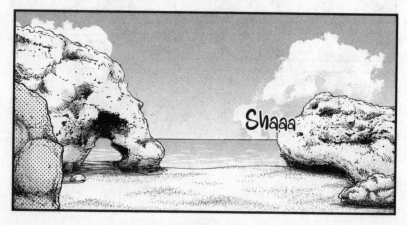

Shaaa

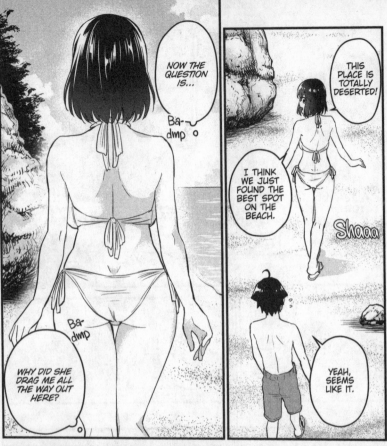

NOW THE QUESTION IS...

Ba-dmp

THIS PLACE IS TOTALLY DESERTED!

I THINK WE JUST FOUND THE BEST SPOT ON THE BEACH.

Shaaa

Ba-dmp

WHY DID SHE DRAG ME ALL THE WAY OUT HERE?

YEAH, SEEMS LIKE IT.

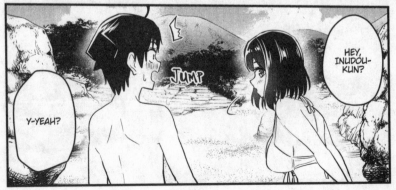

JUMP

Y-YEAH?

HEY, INUDOU-KUN?

WHAT DO YOU THINK ABOUT...
MY BIKINI?
UH, WHAT DO I THINK ABOUT IT...?
IT'S SEXY, FOR STARTERS... WAIT, ABORT THAT LINE OF THOUGHT!
SHE'S JUST SO DAZZLING, MY EYES KEEP WANDERING WHERE THEY SHOULDN'T...
IT'S, UH... ATTRACTIVE? I THINK?
YOU THINK?
Lean

I DON'T MIND.
TAKE A GOOD LOOK.
BA-DMP
ドキ
BA-DMP
ドキ
WUH...

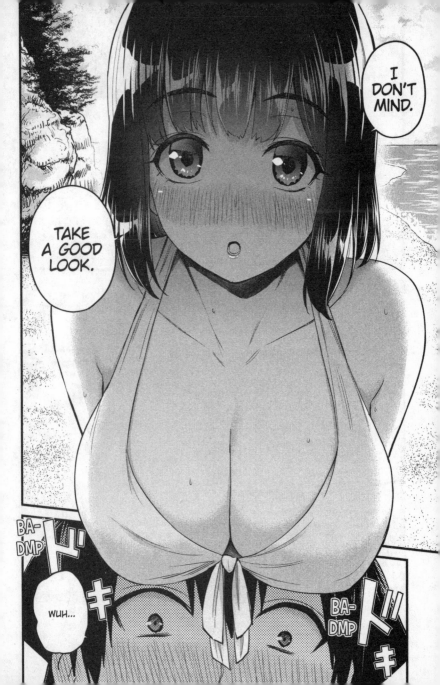

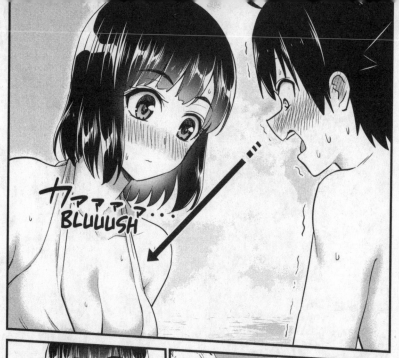

BLUUUSH

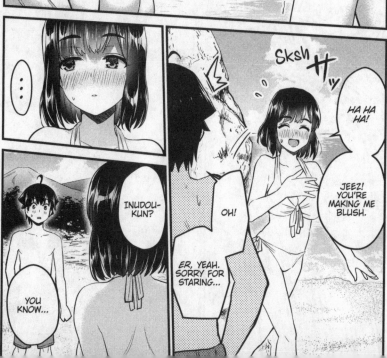

Sksh

HA HA HA!

JEEZ! YOU'RE MAKING ME BLUSH.

OH!

ER, YEAH. SORRY FOR STARING...

INUDOU-KUN?

YOU KNOW...

SPLOOSH
THE TRUTH IS, I...
HUH?
ZLURSH

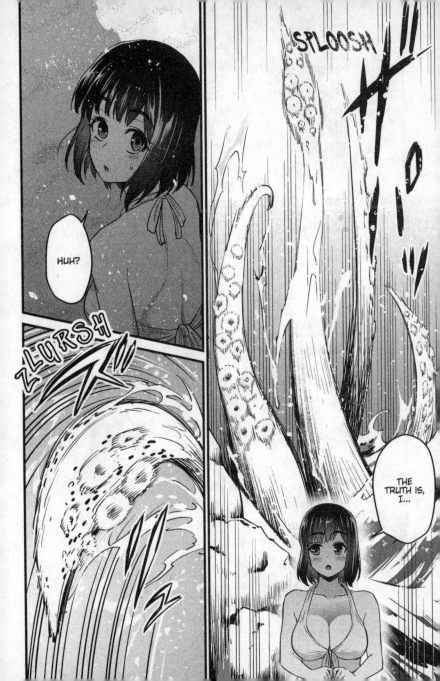

EEEEEK!!
INOSE-SAAAN!!
WHAT IS THAT? A GIANT OCTOPUS? A SQUID?!
EITHER WAY, IT'S A MONSTER!!
Kraken (Demon of the Sea)
HOLD ON, I'LL GET YOU OUT OF THERE!!
DASH
WRIGGLE
WRIGGLE
SHLURM

SPLOOP ♥
Pyah?!
?!
EEP?!
YEEK! WHAT IS IT DOING?!
SCHWOMP ♥
SCHWOMP ♥
THIS SQUID...
SHLOMP
GU HE HE ♥
SHLOMP
IS A MASSIVE PERVERT!!

SHLOOP にゅる♡
?!
OH NO YOU DON'T!!
ズガ GRAB
ぺ
BFFFT!
SHMECK
INOSE-SAN, IT'S NO GOOD! I CAN'T STOP IT!
TRANSFORM INTO A MAGICAL GIRL!
MNUH?
I CAN'T WITHOUT MEPHI-CHAN!
ARGH! SHE NEVER PULLS THROUGH WHEN YOU NEED HER!

にゅるーー!
SLITHER
JOLT
Mngh, no!
Wuh...
Shtop...!
Uhn!
FLINCH
Don't!
SHLOOP

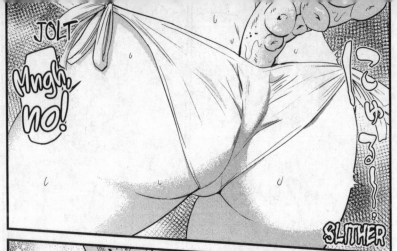

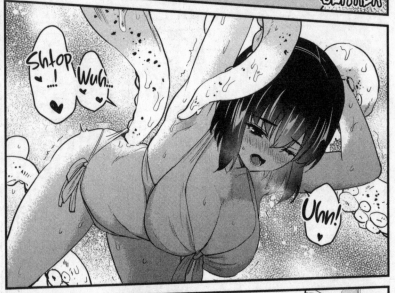

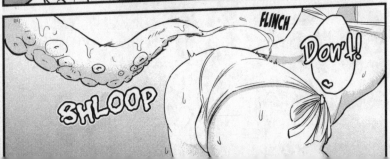

PUCKER
HUFF!
PUCKER
JIGGLE
SHLUP!
Shluuuurp♡
SHUDDER
N...
Nhoooo?!

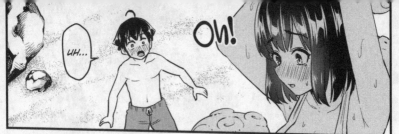

UH... Oh!

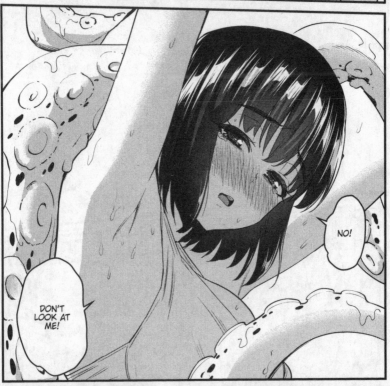

NO!

DON'T LOOK AT ME!

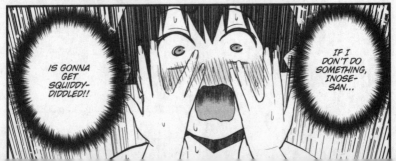

IS GONNA GET SQUIIDDY-DIDDLED!!

IF I DON'T DO SOMETHING, INOSE-SAN...

TCHIING
PLOP
ボト
Tup
ストッ
PLOP
ボト
I THOUGHT I SENSED SOMETHING MALEVOLENT THIS WAY.
SURT-SAN!!

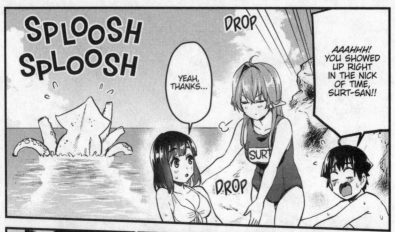

SPLOOSH SPLOOSH

DROP

DROP

YEAH, THANKS...

AAAHHH! YOU SHOWED UP RIGHT IN THE NICK OF TIME, SURT-SAN!!

SURT

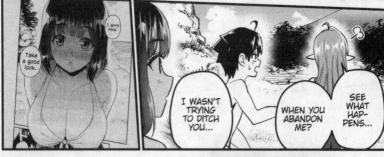

Take a good look.

I don't mind.

I WASN'T TRYING TO DITCH YOU...

WHEN YOU ABANDON ME?

SEE WHAT HAP- PENS...

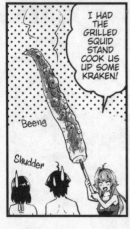

I HAD THE GRILLED SQUID STAND COOK US UP SOME KRAKEN!

Beeng

Shudder

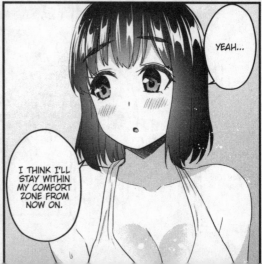

YEAH...

I THINK I'LL STAY WITHIN MY COMFORT ZONE FROM NOW ON.

Does a Hot Elf Live NEXT DOOR to You?

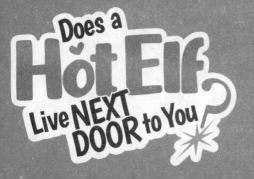

Afterword

And that was volume three! Packed full of romcom subplots, wasn't it? But I have a dark confession to make. I, the author, completely misjudged the pacing of my own series. I thought I could cram one more chapter into this volume, but it had to be pushed back. So much for ending with an Inori cuteness bomb! Jeez. Good job, me!! (Now the rest of volume four gets the challenge of living up to the hype of its first chapter!)

Anyway, a new character appeared this volume.

Is Fafnir too *sexy???*

I'll answer that for you. She ended up being a regular sex bomb. My editor told me to go wild with Fafnir's chapter, so wild I went! What can I say? I like writing those kinds of subplots. This was the first time Inori's shown up in a while, so I had some fun with her, too... Apologies for neglecting our titular heroine, Surt. But I like Inori's character design, so I can't help it! (That, and the advertising wraparound on the Japanese edition featured nothing but black-haired, big-breasted babes with bobs...)

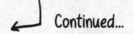 Continued...

↳

I also had Mephi transform(?) into a female! Have you ever seen a character strip naked within two pages of their introduction? That has to be an industry first. I like her, too—she's easy to kick into gear. But she's a demon, so I have to be a little mean to her! She has a history of deceiving our heroines and Inudou, don't forget!
I think that about covers it. I'm having fun with volume four so far, so I hope you all enjoy it, too!

8. 17. 2020

植野 メグル
Meguru Ueno

FAN BOX SPECIAL THANKS

Noga Ken-san
ノガケン さん

Baron-san
バロン さん

Ponta-san
ポンた さん

Mirubii-san
みるびい さん

Minatsuna-san
ミナツナ さん

Sin-san
sin さん

Paul-san
Paul さん

haseo125-san
haseo125 さん

Mizuki Shin-san
水樹慎 さん

& you!!

Thank you for everything!!

Does a **Hot Elf** Live NEXT DOOR to You?

NEXT VOLUME...

The Final Night of School Camp Begins!

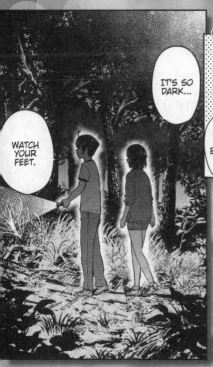

IT'S SO DARK...

WATCH YOUR FEET.

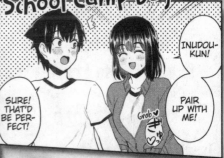

INUDOU-KUN!

PAIR UP WITH ME!

SURE! THAT'D BE PERFECT!

Grab

Inudou and Inose

Pair up for a test of courage ♥

Anything can happen when the lights are out and hearts are racing...

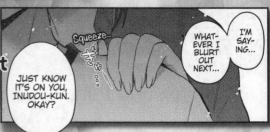

Squeeze...

WHATEVER I BLURT OUT NEXT...

I'M SAYING...

JUST KNOW IT'S ON YOU, INUDOU-KUN. OKAY?

Unbeknownst to Surt
a love triangle forms?!
I LIKE YOU.
INUDOU-KUN.
KISS
Inudou's courage as a man is about to be tested!!
A bevy of otherworldly and superhuman babes push and shove for Inudou's attention!
In the next volume, a delinquent goddess joins the fray, throwing our everyday harem protagonist's life into utter chaos!
Volume 4 Coming Soon!

SEVEN SEAS' GHOST SHIP PRESENTS

Does a Hot Elf Live NEXT DOOR to You?

story and art by MEGURU UENO

VOLUME 3

TRANSLATION	Nicole Frasik
ADAPTATION	Nick Mamatas
LETTERING	Viet Phuong Vu
COVER DESIGN	Nicky Lim
LOGO DESIGN	George Panella
PROOFREADER	B. Lillian Martin
COPY EDITOR	Dawn Davis
EDITOR	Nick Mamatas
PREPRESS TECHNICIAN	Melanie Ujimori
PRINT MANAGER	Rhiannon Rasmussen-Silverstein
PRODUCTION MANAGER - GHOST SHIP	George Panella
PRODUCTION MANAGER	Lissa Pattillo
MANAGING EDITOR	Julie Davis
ASSOCIATE PUBLISHER	Adam Arnold
PUBLISHER	Jason DeAngelis

ISBN: 978-1-64827-511-1
Printed in Canada
First Printing: February 2022
10 9 8 7 6 5 4 3 2 1

READING DIRECTIONS

This book reads from *right to left*, Japanese style. If this is your first time reading manga, you start reading from the top right panel on each page and take it from there. If you get lost, just follow the numbered diagram here. It may seem backwards at first, but you'll get the hang of it! Have fun!!

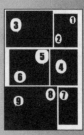

Follow us online: www.GhostShipManga.com